PRAISE FOR

Mom Always Liked

A Guide for Resolving Family Feuds, Inheritance Battles & Eldercare Crises

"This exceptionally wise and immensely practical book provides step-by-step advice that every family needs, as we navigate the challenging transitions of parents' later years. Readers will find useful negotiation and communication advice for resolving many kinds of conflict. By explaining the essentials of negotiation theory in everyday terms, with examples drawn from real cases, the authors have given us a brilliant *Getting to YES* guide for managing family issues."

—David A. Hoffman, Esq.
Boston Law Collaborative, LLC
John H. Watson, Jr. Lecturer on Law at Harvard Law School
Former chair of the American Bar Association Section of Dispute Resolution

"Every family faces challenges, from deciding how to care for elderly parents to figuring out how to divide cherished belongings, and the authors provide guidance on how to work well together. With many stories and examples from their years of experience as mediators, they offer step-by-step instructions for how you and your family can manage conflict, communicate effectively, handle tough situations—and become stronger in the process."

—Susan Hackley
Managing Director, Program on Negotiation at Harvard Law School

"Elder Decisions® has produced an excellent guide for families who are struggling with eldercare decisions. The authors provide a reassuring and practical approach to the process of negotiating and resolving family conflicts. Whether a family is already embroiled in a difficult dispute over Mom or Dad, or just beginning an eldercare journey, it will find words of wisdom in this guide."

—Emily B. Saltz, LICSW, CMC
Director, Elder Resources
Board Member, National Association of Professional Geriatric Care Managers

"Elder care challenges can be the petri dishes of family conflict. Fortunately, this new book by the leading elder mediators at Elder Decisions® provides the antidote. I hope that families all over will use the methods it prescribes to r

—Harry S. Margolis, Esq.
Margolis & Bloom, LLP
under of ElderLawAnswers.com

Mom Always Liked You Best

A Guide for Resolving Family Feuds, Inheritance Battles & Eldercare Crises

ARLINE KARDASIS

RIKK LARSEN

CRYSTAL THORPE

BLAIR TRIPPE

Copyright © 2011
Elder Decisions®, a division of Agreement Resources, LLC
By Arline Kardasis, Rikk Larsen, Crystal Thorpe, Blair Trippe

All rights reserved. No part of this publication may be reproduced,
stored in a retrieval system, or transmitted, in any form or by any means,
electronic, mechanical, photocopying, recording, or otherwise,
without the written permission of Agreement Resources, LLC.

48236185 3/12

ISBN-13: 978-0615480886
ISBN-10: 0615480888

Design: Friskey Design

www.ElderDecisions.com
www.AgreementResources.com

Dedicated to our clients,
who have opened their hearts to us,
and to our families,
who have supported us
every step of the way

IS THIS GUIDE FOR YOU?

Are you one of the millions of Americans currently struggling with adult family conflict? Is your family trying to manage an ongoing dispute around eldercare, family property, estate planning, or inheritance issues? Is your family conflict causing distress for your elderly parent? Do you love your siblings but have no idea how to get them to communicate and make decisions?

When you are impacted by ongoing conflict, it can seem very dark out there. If your family is experiencing these or any other all too common adult family challenges, we invite you to read on.

These days, families live very complicated lives, and it is normal for them to face conflict. We have helped many such families around the United States and Canada and want you to know that there is hope for a positive resolution. We wrote this guide to give you and your family members the tools needed to achieve those mutual agreements that seem so elusive right now.

You might be wondering who we are and why we think we can teach you about conflict resolution. We are adult family mediators (also known as "elder mediators") and conflict coaches. We work with families who are in conflict around elder transitions and associated issues. This is specialized work, and we are "thought leaders" in the field, having provided training for mediators from the United States, Canada, Europe and Australia. In addition to our expertise as elder mediators, our team of professionals has decades of experience in the areas of education, finance, healthcare, social work, and estate settlement, as well as our own family experiences.

With our aging population, conflict is a growing problem in families. Fortunately, the field of conflict resolution has developed practical skills for resolving family conflict, and these skills are now being taught in academic, professional and community-based programs around the world. By reading this guide and practicing the techniques that we lay out for you in the chapters ahead, you can learn skills used by trained professionals.

In the pages ahead, you will learn tools to help you stop having those circular arguments that go on interminably and get you nowhere. We hope that you will use this guide to empower yourself to think like a mediator in order to become a better decision-maker, a more mindful negotiator, and a more effective communicator. Our goal is to help you to lead your own family members toward consensus around some of the most important decisions you will ever face together.

CONTENTS

INTRODUCTION

There's a new reality for families today characterized by a dramatic increase in adult family conflict. Many adult siblings are having a difficult time as they face their parents' aging and related decisions regarding caregiving, healthcare, property distribution, estate planning, and more. And it is now common for us to live at a distance from our aging parents and siblings. This can lead to a breakdown in family communication and increased conflict over important, often critical, family decisions.

Do you know anyone who is in the middle of a fight over family assets or vacation homes? We hear about celebrity families in the midst of such conflict, but there are many thousands more who are not in the spotlight. While, in the abstract, the challenges of sharing family homes and assets seem like nice problems to have, these dilemmas account for some of the most vicious family feuds and court battles in our society. Sibling wealth disparity and the division of family assets is one of the leading causes of strife in families today. Rivalries, jealousies and the quest for fairness play out in living rooms and dining rooms in our neighborhoods, and perhaps even in your home.

In our work as elder mediators we see many themes repeat themselves over and over again. The most common triggers of family conflict are:

- Asset distribution including homes, land, antiques, artwork, and more

- Caregiving for elderly family members

- Old relationship patterns and unhealed wounds that are still being worked out among siblings and between parents and their adult children

- Geographic dispersion and infrequent communication

- Sibling wealth disparity

Caregiving responsibilities, as mentioned above, are a major source of family conflict. In the United States alone, over 43 million people serve as unpaid caregivers of adults who are 50 years or older, involving about a quarter or more of U.S. households, according to *Caregiving in the US 2009,* by the National Alliance for Caregiving in collaboration with AARP. This report reveals that over 30% of caregivers provide care for five years or more, and while the majority of caregivers are woman, one third of American caregivers are men. But being one of many doesn't make the burden of caregiving any easier to deal with. While approximately 80% of us have siblings, most of us feel we're shouldering this awesome responsibility alone.

American adults are now living on average until age 78, three decades longer than they did a century ago, and many of our parents are living past 90. With modern medicine, they are able to live with chronic diseases that often require some degree of ongoing care. And with further advances in medical treatments, the number of people living well into their 80s needing increasing amounts of care will only grow.

So it's likely that most of us will face challenges within our own families as the years go by. When we need to make difficult decisions or when family members can't agree on how to move forward on issues relating to an aging parent or an inheritance matter, productive family discussions, which sometimes include a facilitator or mediator, are essential. These discussions often focus on values, relationships, trust, and fairness, as well as the interests of the elder and of the adult siblings and their families.

In the pages ahead, we will share with you the techniques that skilled mediators use to open up the lines of communication and to explore opportunities for collaboration and consensus building among family members. When you're finished reading this guide, we hope you will pass it on to your family members so that you can begin to speak the language of conflict resolution together. There is nothing you can't accomplish when you work as a team—communicating, making decisions, and solving problems in new and more effective ways. And since we hope you will want to continue to learn more, we've included a resource section at the end of the book that offers suggestions of where to go for more specific topical information.

1

NAVIGATING YOUR WAY THROUGH THE CONFLICT

Being in conflict with someone, especially with a family member, is disorienting. When we're in a dispute, we feel lost—we're on a journey we do not control. Navigating from where we are to where we think we want to go is almost impossible because others keep putting up roadblocks. Plus, everyone is coming from different places, and there is no consensus on the final destination. So how does a family find its way? We need some guidance before the dispute hijacks our family relationships taking us to some desolate place or landing us in a ditch.

YOUR *CONFLICT RESOLUTION GPS*

Many of us have learned to love the *GPS* in our car because it guides us to our destination and it helps us to avoid all the wasted time we used to spend being lost. Wouldn't it be great if you could employ a reliable system like a *GPS* to help you navigate the terrain of a family dispute? You can! Your *Conflict Resolution GPS* is a tool that can provide you with a system for understanding where you are, how you got there, and ultimately where you want to go. You can use this tool for yourself, and to help others with whom you are at odds. Then, together, you will be able to better understand each other.

To see how the *Conflict Resolution GPS* works, consider the following family dispute:

Two sisters, Ellen and Susan, have been sharing the costs of maintaining the old family vacation house on Cape Cod for five years, since Dad finished gifting the property to them equally, retaining a $^1/_3$ interest for himself. Dad is not able to make the trip from his New Hampshire home to the Cape anymore. Ellen wants to sell the house or have Susan buy her out. She lives in Florida and rarely, if ever, brings her family there. On the other hand, Susan is adamant that the house should be kept in the family and she claims that she cannot afford to buy Ellen out. Susan uses the house every summer and is furious that Ellen wants to sell the old place.

Dad is ready to redo his estate plan, and he is worried about this ongoing dispute concerning the house. Nobody is sure what outcome he would prefer, but everyone is aware of how deeply saddened he is by the conflict. It's troubling to him to see his two daughters at odds, and he is upset that the gift of this wonderful house is turning into a family nightmare. He finds it too difficult to face the conflict, and he knows that Mom would have been heartbroken had she lived to see this turn of events. Dad wants Ellen and Susan to figure it out and let him know their plan. He says that he will not try to influence the outcome. Really, he just wants them to get along so he doesn't feel caught in the middle.

With that scenario in mind, let's look at your new tool—your *Conflict Resolution GPS*, where *GPS* stands for *Guiding Positions to Solutions*. This tool can help you navigate from *positions* (those conclusions and demands that fuel your disputes) to *solutions* (those well considered and mutually agreeable resolutions to which you aspire).

Drawn from the *Ladder of Inference* model, originally developed by Chris Argyris, your *Conflict Resolution GPS* will reveal—through a three-step process—how you and others arrive at and get stuck in your conclusions. In a nutshell, it looks like this:

STEP 1: Observations

The world around us provides infinite information from which we consciously or unconsciously select what we will actually take in (our data points). It's a huge and confusing map, so we select what seems important or what has captured our attention and we move on from there. In order to figure out how we got to our conflicting conclusions in a dispute, we need to first consider exactly what information we have each observed and chosen as reliable. That's the first step on our journey.

STEP 2: Internal Processing / Interpretations

Once we take in our selected observations, we pass them through our own personal editing system (our reference maps). This editing system works subconsciously using our past experiences, knowledge, biases, assumptions, fears, values, needs, and desires. With our personal editing system, we interpret our selected observations. That's the second step on our journey.

STEP 3: Drawing Conclusions / Taking a Stand

Taking a stand is Step 3—this is our "position," and it is often where we find ourselves at odds with family members and others. Our conclusions are the result of our Steps 1 and 2. We have selected and taken in information, and we have processed it through our own editing system resulting in our stated opinion, our position. Because our positions make complete sense to us and are often viewed as non-negotiable, it's not surprising that conversations with others who took their own journey become so difficult. We find it virtually impossible to reconcile where each of us is and where we want to go because, like us, they took seemingly logical steps and have chosen data which they processed and interpreted to form their own, independent conclusions.

So, we can see how Ellen and Susan arrived at different conclusions about what to do with the family beach house if we use our *Conflict Resolution GPS* to walk through the three-step process they each used.

Remember, Ellen's position is that the family vacation home at the beach should be sold sooner rather than later. She believes that this is the best possible solution to their ongoing dispute. But her sister Susan wants to keep the house in the family. These are two very different positions. However, they both agree on one thing—they want to stop arguing about this since their father is clear that he wants them to come up with a plan.

Let's look at Ellen's stated position that the house must be sold. Why does she insist on this? First, she does not think it is fair that she is paying a share of the taxes and the high costs of maintaining this aging property. And she could use the cash from a buyout. This has been a tough few years for her financially, and she figures that her portion of the equity would be substantial. Her conclusion seems well-considered to her, and she is not likely to waver.

Ellen thinks Susan is unreasonable—her sister goes on and on about the memories and the family heritage that this home represents. Ellen understands the sentimentality, but why should she have to support Susan's summer vacations? If Susan wants to take her kids to Cape Cod and keep the memories alive, Ellen figures they should just get the house appraised and Susan should pay Ellen her fair share.

Susan, on the other hand, is very distressed by this entire matter. She can't even contemplate selling the house that has been the one constant in the family. She is also worried that the mere mention of selling the property is upsetting Dad. Even if he says he doesn't care what she and Ellen decide, she strongly believes that he will be devastated if the house is sold outside the family, and she is in no position to buy her sister out at this time.

Before they can start to discuss possibilities for resolution, they'll want to begin to understand how they might have each gotten to such different places. Let's see how they might use the *Conflict Resolution GPS* tool.

ELLEN'S PROCESS:

STEP 1: Observations

Ellen has not been to Cape Cod in eight years, and her kids barely remember the place. She lives on the beach in Florida and goes to her cabin in the mountains of North Carolina for summer vacations. Susan, on the other hand, brings her family to the old house on weekends throughout the year and sometimes takes up residence for as long as three weeks during the summer.

Ellen knows that the house is owned free and clear by the three of them in equal parts, and she believes that it would be worth just over a million dollars. So, she figures her share would be at least $333,000.

Her kids are fast approaching their college years. Sadly, she doesn't have much of a nest egg as the market downturn was a disaster for her.

STEP 2: Internal Processing / Interpretations

It just seems completely unfair for her to continue to pay taxes and upkeep on this property. She feels that by doing nothing she is funding her sister's vacations. Ellen believes that fairness means something much closer to equal usage. She has no need for a beach house in New England and just wants to get her money out of it.

STEP 3: Drawing Conclusions / Taking a Stand

Based on Steps 1 and 2, Ellen concludes that the house must be sold or else she needs to be bought out. The conclusion that her family should sell the house is based on her **observations** (she doesn't have significant savings to pay for college, her share in the house is valued at over $333,000, and she isn't making use of the house) and her **interpretations** (she needs money, the only way she can imagine getting any value from the house is to sell her share, and the current situation is not fair). Giving up her share of the house makes perfect sense to her; she feels that she's been very thoughtful, generous, and appropriate. . . and it's all very logical. Who could argue with that?

SUSAN'S PROCESS:

As it turns out, Susan has been using her own *Conflict Resolution GPS* and would claim that she too has been thoughtful, generous, and appropriate in her thinking. From her vantage point, her position also is very simple and reasonable. Let's take a look at how she got here.

STEP 1: Observations

Susan's fondest memories are tied to that house! She was very close to Mom, and they spent many summers there together planting the gardens, making decorations for the 4th of July, planning neighborhood clambakes, and enjoying the long stretches of beach in the early morning. Susan even got married at the beach house.

Ellen has always complained about money, but she seems to live very well. And Susan has not forgotten that she generously helped Ellen out with moving costs when Ellen relocated to Florida after losing her job.

Yes, it's true that Ellen rarely uses the house and she claims to be stretched financially. Susan has considered the possibility of buying her out but she really doesn't see how she could pull it off.

STEP 2: Internal Processing / Interpretations

Even the thought of selling the house makes Susan cry. She's always assumed her children would get married there, and she knows if the house were sold, it would be devastating to her father. She just can't believe her sister would consider this.

From her perspective, Ellen can use the house anytime she wants. The fact that she doesn't choose to doesn't make Susan responsible for paying Ellen's share or buying her out.

And she feels it just wouldn't be right to ask Dad to chip in—after all, the house was a gift from him.

Susan is sure that Ellen can't sell without her acquiescence, but this ongoing fight is unpleasant and exhausting.

Lastly, Susan feels that she has always been the one to pick up the pieces for Ellen, and she is tired of it.

STEP 3: Drawing Conclusions / Taking a Stand

By going through the process, Susan concludes that the house must not be sold under any circumstances; it must be kept in the family. This conclusion is based on her **observations** (the house holds a lot of memories, she doesn't currently have the funds to buy her sister out, etc.) and her **interpretations** (her sister can use the house any time she wants, selling it would be traumatic for Dad, and of course her children will want to get married there, etc.).

Keeping the house makes perfect sense to her; she feels that she's been very thoughtful, generous, and appropriate... and it's all very logical. Who could argue with that?

Despite their differing conclusions, Ellen and Susan agree that they need to get on the same page in order to settle this once and for all. This has already been too upsetting for them and for their father.

So where do they begin in their efforts to come together? They begin at Step 1 on their individual *GPS* journey. This is where they can discuss exactly what they have observed. Have they focused on different data? Can they enlarge one another's field of view? Once they agree on what observations can be included in their discussion, they can explore how they have each interpreted their observations. Did they make assumptions? Can they work together to either verify or debunk these assumptions? What has led them to the conclusions they have each come to? Are they weighing information in light of personal values or past experiences in their own lives? Might other values and experiences lead them to different conclusions?

With the *GPS* as their tool, let's see what a productive conversation the sisters could have rather than rehashing the same old arguments.

> **ELLEN:** *You know, we've been going back and forth on this for a long time. I'd really like to understand more about why you are so adamant about my remaining as a partner in the house.*

> **SUSAN:** *I just don't want to lose the house. It has generations of memories, and Dad and Mom both wanted us to keep it for our children—and I had always hoped my kids would be married there. I know that you don't use the house, and I realize that you are not likely to do so. But I would like us to figure out a way to keep it in the family.*

> **ELLEN:** *I'm not saying you can't do that—I'm just saying it doesn't make sense for me right now to pay all the expenses for a house I never use.*

> **SUSAN:** *I know that, but it doesn't mean we have to sell it. I wish I could just write you a check today for your share, but that's just not possible. We're in this together and need to figure out a way to make it work.*

> **ELLEN:** *I get that and I don't disagree with any of that. Tell me how you see me figuring into this.*

SUSAN: *You are part of the history of the house and part of its future as well. I know that the monthly payments seem excessive, given that you don't use the place, but I would hope that we could come up with a way to offset those payments. I was thinking about renting the house out during the summer months. It's a great location, and the neighbors get huge weekly rates for their houses. I've been talking with them, and they told me all about the vacation rental website that they use to advertise their properties. I actually think we could turn a profit and end up more than covering our costs.*

ELLEN: *But I thought you used the house in the summer months.*

SUSAN: *I do, but maybe we could figure out the value of the time I used the house and reduce your financial obligations accordingly. Would that seem fair to you?*

ELLEN: *Let me think about that. Someone would have to manage the housekeeping, advertising, and all that.*

SUSAN: *I know. I'd be willing to do that.*

ELLEN: *It never occurred to me that you would be willing to manage summer rentals. But, Susan, the other piece of this is that I'd like to get my money out, you know that.*

SUSAN: *Yes, I do, but here's what I'd like you to consider. Dad may say he doesn't care what we decide, but I believe he would be heartbroken if we sold the house. I've spoken with him about it and although he says we should do what's best for us, he'd be thrilled if we could figure out a way to keep it in the family. Besides, I just can't afford to buy out your share right now.*

I'm wondering if you would consider holding on and not forcing a sale as long as Dad is alive. I have some ideas for improvements on the property that would increase its value down the line. I could cover the costs of the improvements now, and you could repay me later out of your equity—either when the house is sold or when I buy out your share, if I am able to do so. And, no one can predict what might remain in Dad's estate after he passes. It is possible that we will inherit enough that it won't be necessary to sell the house. I might be able to buy you out then, or you might no longer wish to sell your share.

ELLEN: *So you're suggesting that we turn the house into a source of income and that we hold onto it for its future value. What makes you think this will work?*

They continue to talk about the research Susan has already done and the information they will need to gather before making any final decisions. Ellen shares a bit about her financial situation (she never thought she would do that), and Susan realizes that she may need to consider buying out some portion of Ellen's ownership in the near future.

The conversation focuses on reviewing each of their observations and interpretations, and they agree to some ways to gather more information before reaching any new conclusions. The sisters are beginning to think like a team and are in a much better place to approach Dad and have a productive conversation as a family.

OK, so you "get it," and you are impressed that Ellen and Susan so easily conducted a fruitful conversation. But you remain skeptical about your own family's capacity to do this. We ask you to be patient. Ellen and Susan had other tools and training to support their improved communications. Please read on.

—•—

The *GPS* tool teaches us to think like investigators and then to share our observations and interpretations with our potential collaborators. By working together to explore our observations, to consider the validity of our assumptions, and to determine what additional information or advice might be helpful, we can zoom in on some details or step back to look at the bigger picture. We can share our observations in a clearer way as we begin to feel less lost and much further along the road to agreement.

2

....

USING YOUR *GPS* TO SEPARATE INTERESTS FROM POSITIONS

Our clients come to us because their families are at an impasse in their efforts to make important decisions. These decisions can pertain to any number of issues. Family members may be embroiled in a painful dispute around estate and inheritance issues. Or siblings may be concerned about the health and safety of an elder. Maybe Dad's car has dents of unknown origin, or Mom has been donating large amounts of money to a charity that no one has ever heard of. Sometimes adult siblings are concerned because they have found Mom's house uncharacteristically cluttered and they are worried about her ability to manage the house and pay the bills, or because she has been spending lots of time with a man who recently moved to the area. Family members may be exhausted and frustrated beyond words. In their conversations with us, they often let us know that they are "feeling lost" and they don't know how to proceed.

When family members don't have an internal *GPS* to guide them they often turn to us, as mediators, to help them find a path from impasse to resolution. If your family is not likely to participate in mediation, you can activate your own *GPS* and employ some of the skills and tools that we share in this chapter and beyond.

SEPARATING INTERESTS FROM POSITIONS

One of the most important skills that a mediator can offer to his or her clients is an ability to help them to think about their *interests*, including their needs, wishes, values, aspirations, fears, and concerns. Most people arrive at mediation having well-crafted *positions*—these are their conclusions, their opinions, their one proposed solution, their "non-negotiables," and so on.

Let's look at an example with "your" family....

Your position may be that Mom should stop driving—immediately. You might even have figured out how to achieve this: You will take the battery out of her car. Doing so would accomplish the goal of your position—"Mom cannot drive anymore." But you may not have given much thought to what is behind that position—your interests. And you are even less likely to have considered the interests of the other participants in the dispute.

If you break down the situation, your interests may include ensuring Mom's safety and the safety of others on the roadways; keeping Mom from driving would accomplish that. But, in truth, there's a lot going on. In addition to your safety concerns, you also are worried about Mom's ability to maintain her social life without driving. You may also want to be sure that your mother maintains her dignity and her sense of independence, as well as her quality of life. And you don't want her to be upset and angry with you.

At the same time, your sister Amanda might hold the position that Mom is fine and should be able to continue driving and that she will suffer enormously if you try to make her stop driving. Behind that position, she has several interests that might include her concern for Mom's well-being; she thinks Mom may become depressed and lonely if she can't drive around. Amanda may also worry about how personally inconvenienced she will be if Mom needs to be driven everywhere.

Often, when people are facing tough decisions and they disagree about the best way to proceed, arguments ensue regarding who's right or wrong based on the "facts." These perceived "facts" are often individual conclusions, and they simply harden our positions: "Mom will be depressed if she can't drive"; "Those dents were not there last month"; "Mom will hurt herself or someone else if she continues driving." These may or may not be accurate claims, and they often contribute to impasse as family members hold tight to their own assertions and dismiss those of others. You can imagine how this becomes even more difficult as more people are involved. The conversation becomes about perceived facts, not about what's really important to each person—their interests.

A conversation about interests provides many more opportunities for collaborative decision-making: "I want Mom to be safe"; "I'd like Mom to keep her social connections"; "I don't want to be a daily taxi service for Mom." We help our clients separate their interests from their positions. And you can learn how to do this for yourself and for others in your family.

Why should you care about interests? Mainly because you can't often get to a lasting solution from a position without first understanding the underlying reasons that resulted in that stance. Even if two people have diametrically opposed positions, there may be some common interests that can be well-served by a solution that works for both. You are much more likely to create a successful resolution for yourself and your family if everyone has identified their own and others' interests because you will be able to see where commonalities exist. From there, you can create a resolution that meets those interests to the greatest extent possible.

Most people believe that a good outcome means convincing others that they are right in the hope of achieving everything they stipulated in their starting demands. Yet, true success is achieved only when you have determined what you need and why—and when you have created a resolution that satisfies your needs regardless of whether the resolution matches your initially stated position.

To separate a position from an interest, think about the "why" in every position statement. If you believe that Mom needs to stop driving right away, you should be asking yourself "why?" You have seen the dents on her car, and you were horrified when she admitted that she got lost driving home last week. The interests that will emerge may include Mom's safety, your own kids' safety when she drives them around, and your responsibility to the community. If you are honest with yourself, you may also acknowledge that you are tired of worrying about this and you just want the worry to go away. At the same time, you have a nagging concern about how Mom will cope without her car, since you do still want her to maintain her autonomy and keep up her social relationships. However, you have not really figured out any details of how Mom might get around without driving so that she can continue to live the full life that she is accustomed to.

If Amanda says that Mom is fine driving, ask her to help you understand what her thoughts are. What has she observed? What concerns, if any, does she have regarding the dents or Mom's getting lost?

If you inquire in a respectful and genuinely curious manner, Amanda may reveal that she has seen some dents on the car, but she doesn't want to upset Mom by asking her about them, although she knows something's not right. She may also articulate that, like you, she just can't imagine how Mom can maintain her full life without her car.

You may soon see that you and Amanda actually share some of the same interests. You can both agree that you care deeply about Mom's happiness, and you worry that she would suffer if she could not continue an active life with her committees and her bridge game. You also agree that safety is important—but you are not certain about how risky it is for her to be driving. In addition, you both recognize that plans will have to be made about substitute transportation if Mom is no longer driving.

Once you have established that you share these common interests (Mom's happiness, her safety, and her independence), you are ready to work together to get the information you need and to plan next steps with the goal of addressing all the interests you have been discussing together.

GATHERING MORE INFORMATION

In situations like this, often the first order of business for adult siblings in their efforts to find resolution is to identify what they want to achieve and then to agree on what information is needed and who will research it. Information gathering is a way to begin the teamwork necessary to make informed decisions in a collaborative manner. Once interests have been identified, it's important to put aside positions and collect the needed information before coming to a resolution. Trying to stick with a position "on principle" doesn't help the situation at all. We'll talk about this more in the next chapter.

If this were your family, you and Amanda could share the work of investigating driving assessment programs. Depending upon where your mother lives, you might contact her state Department of Motor Vehicles, local police department or areas hospitals to ask for help. In exploring alternative means of transportation for Mom, different communities have different resources, so you might look into the costs of local taxi services and the availability of vans run by the senior center. You would also want to decide how best to approach Mom. Sometimes it works best to have a trusted doctor discuss driving concerns during a planned office visit.

So—the decision is far more complex and nuanced than "take away the keys or remove the battery" vs. "leave her alone." You and Amanda have uncovered a variety of common interests, and you can now work as a team to create some possible solutions that address these interests. And most important, together you can use the same process to check-in with Mom about her interests as well.

————

Positions are our conclusions—they are clear and definite. Interests are what lie below—why we feel the way we do. Positions don't lend themselves to open discussions about solutions. They paint people into corners and hinder their ability to think broadly about the situation at hand. When someone is positional, respectfully ask them why they feel that way. The answer to the "why" question will become the basis of the solutions you can develop together.

3

....

CURIOSITY AND ACTIVE LISTENING

L et's say that you and your brother Peter are constantly arguing about where your father should be living. You know that this needs to be addressed, and you believe that it is important for the two of you to each understand where the other is coming from before talking with Dad about your concerns.

Now that you understand the importance of uncovering your own interests and those of others rather than butting heads over positions and conclusions, you'd like to have a conversation with Peter where you talk about interests—but you don't know how to approach your brother without getting caught up in the usual heated exchanges. How can you make him listen to you and understand what you are hoping to achieve? He's so pig headed!

First, you will want to think about your own goals. You say that you'd like to understand your brother's thinking. But if you are honest with yourself, you might acknowledge that you have little hope of learning anything new from him. You've had many fruitless conversations, and you have reached the conclusion that he is out of touch (or selfish, or mean spirited, or dysfunctional—you can fill in the blanks). You may feel like there is nothing more to talk about with him until he comes to his senses and accepts your way of thinking. Does this sound familiar?

Stop here. Before you can hope to have a productive conversation, you need to be open to the possibility that your brother may have interests which are actually logical, well intentioned, and informed by observations and experiences about which you may have little or no knowledge. Your first job is to be curious about this, genuinely curious. Does this sound impossible? Are you thinking that you are beyond your capacity to feel or express curiosity? Maybe you can't bear to listen to him anymore. It's time for *him* to listen to *you*! Right? This may be your position at the moment, but let's see if it serves your interests. . . .

What we know for sure is that most people cannot truly listen to someone else's point of view until and unless they feel that they have been respectfully listened to themselves. This is especially true when there has been ongoing conflict. Often no one is listening and no one is feeling heard when family members are at impasse.

So the best strategy for you is to bite your lip and be the first one to do the listening, because you are wise enough to know that—not only might you learn something—this is also how you will be successful in ultimately being heard by Peter. And the best way to listen well is to be genuinely curious and to use the **Active Listening** techniques we are about to suggest.

In order to exhibit genuine curiosity, you must convince yourself that there might be something new and worthwhile to learn from the other person. If you are approaching the topic with open curiosity and are truly listening for clues as to why someone has reached a particular conclusion, then you can become the active listener that you want to be.

SETTING YOUR *GPS* TO "ACTIVE LISTENING"

To best satisfy your new-found curiosity, you now need to set your *GPS* to Active Listening. (*This is likely a new route for you to take, and you will need to watch the road carefully and read all the signs to stay on course. Let's give it a spin.*)

WHY IS ACTIVE LISTENING IMPORTANT?

When practicing Active Listening, you are working very hard to fully understand another person's interests. Initially, everything you are doing is directed toward this goal, and this full understanding will serve your purposes in the long run.

While you are attempting to understand someone else's interests, make a point of checking in with the other person to make sure that you are "getting it" and that they feel both heard and understood. You will need to let them know that you have understood their concerns, their desires, their sense of fairness—all the interests that they have expressed to you. Don't just assume that a little head nodding will do the trick. We'll show you what we mean as we get into the specific tools that you can draw upon in Active Listening.

One of the benefits of Active Listening is that it allows us to uncover a spectrum of feelings at play in another person's emotional state—not just one or two headline feelings. Of course you have noticed that sometimes when we are fearful or sad, we get frustrated and angry, and the emotion that takes the lead is anger. That's what others see and respond to. In Active Listening, you will use your skills to dig below the surface emotion—the blaring headline display—and uncover a wide range of feelings, such as: fear, grief, even love!

Have you ever seen someone yelling at a child for misbehaving? Maybe the little boy just climbed on top of a woodpile, after being warned countless times of the dangers. His father is in a rage, furious that the child has disobeyed him. What you might see is yelling, arms waving, threats, and even physical roughness as he picks the boy up and brings him inside the house. This sure looks like anger, and that certainly is the headline emotion. But, what lies beneath? Fear, of course. The father is scared that the boy will slip and the woodpile will crumble, crushing his foot, or worse. Furthermore, he is concerned that if his son will disobey him right before his eyes, what might he do when unattended? All the "what ifs" are colliding in his mind and creating a brew of worry. If we continue to explore the father's emotions, we realize that this fear is being fueled by his love for his son. It is the love that engages him so deeply. So we see a headline emotion of anger, even rage, but we can't really understand what is going on if we don't dig deeper.

In dealing with adult families in conflict, we find that anger and frustration among siblings may be easy for them to express, but the worries and the emotional needs that lie below often take time and trust to be revealed. If a sibling is angry about shouldering a disproportionate share of the caregiving responsibilities for an aging parent, she may have been able to talk about her anger, but she might not have expressed that she is worried about losing her mother and dealing with terrible grief; that she is sad that her sister has not shown any appreciation for all her work and dedication to THEIR mother; that she feels unloved by her brother who never calls her, even on her birthday; and that she feels guilty that she didn't do more for their father when he was ill. In Active Listening, we hope to open up the channels for communicating these feeling and enriching the conversation by revealing authentic interests.

As a good listener, you can set a positive tone for a conversation by being engaged, non-judgmental, and respectful, and in the process you'll also be modeling good listening skills for others. If you can bring these skills to your family discussions, you can elicit more information; uncover underlying interests, feelings, and perceptions; and you can start the process of building or rebuilding trust.

Active Listening enables people to feel heard and acknowledged so they can move towards problem solving. And remember, your family members will be better able to hear you and understand your story after they feel heard.

DEVELOPING YOUR OWN ACTIVE LISTENING SKILLS

As we go over the skills that are most useful for Active Listening, we want to remind you of the goals of Active Listening: to fully understand others' interests, to create trust, to show respect, to allow others to tell their story and vent their emotions, to provide a safe environment that encourages others to think about and reveal their interests, and ultimately to foster creative problem solving.

YOUR ACTIVE LISTENING KIT:
THE 10 INSTRUMENTS FOR PRODUCTIVE CONVERSATIONS

1. The Conversation Booster
2. Acknowledging and Showing Appreciation
3. Asking Clarifying Questions
4. Summarizing
5. Reframing
6. Using Technology Wisely
7. Introducing Optimism
8. Using Transparency
9. Using "And" Instead of "But"
10. Avoiding Toxic Questions and Comments

There are, as you will see, many techniques that you can employ in your efforts to become a skillful active listener. You may find that some of these approaches come naturally to you. If so, that's great! Build on these first and be mindful of your strategies—then try less familiar ones—see what works and what doesn't work in a particular situation.

With practice, you will discover that you have a variety of tools in your kit, and you can become quite agile and adept at utilizing them. Over time, you will find them to be useful in any conversation, in a variety of settings—whether with family, friends, or colleagues. They can be especially helpful when used in the context of family meetings, to be discussed more in Chapter 10.

1. THE "CONVERSATION BOOSTER"
The greatest tool for peace building!

> You need to set the right tone as you begin the conversation so give considerable attention to how you start. We find it best to begin with a broad, open-ended question like, "So, where should we begin?" This allows others to start wherever they feel comfortable and to take the lead in setting the direction of the conversation. Remember, your turn will come later.
>
> A conversation booster is a question or comment that has no hidden agenda but certainly has an important purpose. It's simply an invitation to someone to tell you more about <u>whatever they wish to talk about.</u> By using conversation boosters, you show that you are curious and anxious to learn as much as possible from others. The responses you receive will often surprise you.
>
> Conversation boosters are usually short, like:
> - "What else?"
> - "Really? Why?"
> - "Tell me more."
> - "Go on."
>
> These little gems encourage others to elaborate, add additional details, and express emotions; they can ultimately be all that is needed for people to honestly speak about their underlying interests.

A conversation booster is nearly always taken as a welcome sign of genuine curiosity. People are usually pleasantly surprised when they are encouraged to "go on." When was the last time anyone invited you to expand on what you were saying? The message that comes through is: *"You've got the floor. I want to hear everything."* Most people will appreciate your expression of curiosity as long as it is delivered in an authentic and modest manner.

Remember that the goal of these inquiries is to focus on interests—on what's really important to someone else and why. It is not the time for you to defend yourself or your actions or to dispute the accuracy of facts. After you have uncovered someone's interests (*"I care about Mom being safe and, of course, I want her to be happy"*), then you will be ready to talk about proposals for resolution. We'll discuss this more in the next chapter.

2. ACKNOWLEDGING AND SHOWING APPRECIATION

When someone has indicated that they are angry or worried or generally unhappy with a situation (or with you!), you can reflect back what you have heard and acknowledge the emotion. Actually name it. Your goal here is to let the other person know that you realize that they are angry, or sad, or fearful. Here you can show empathy (not necessarily agreement). You might simply say: "I can see that you are frustrated with me, and I know that this situation has been hard on you." This shows that you get it without indicating that you agree with their position. Once you are able to empathize, you can begin to have a discussion that uncovers interests. And, when you generously provide acknowledgement, you will be much more likely to receive some in return—at some point.

One important caveat: After you tell someone that you can see how upset they are with you, be sure to resist the urge to justify your actions with "but I don't think it's as bad as you are making it out to be." This will only erase the good you accomplished when you acknowledged their emotions.

Expressing your appreciation for someone's participation in a difficult conversation can go a long way toward building trust. You can simply say that you realize that the discussion is hard for her (or for *"both of us"*) and that you are grateful that she has been willing to try to work things out with you. Appreciation can be very powerful as long as it is offered sincerely.

Reflecting emotions and acknowledging others' difficulties sets a tone of respect. It shows that you are open to considering their feelings. It also lets others know that you have been paying careful attention and that you are invested in the process. The rewards for you will come later.

3. ASKING CLARIFYING QUESTIONS (CAREFULLY)

After you have encouraged someone to tell you what's on his mind, you can show that you are truly curious about his interests by asking for details. "How?", "When?", or "Where?" can be included in your questions following his sweeping statements. So, when your brother says, "I think Dad's estate was unfairly distributed, and I think that I am entitled to way more than I got!" You might simply respond, "Paul, I hear how upset you are; can you tell me what in particular seems unfair to you? I am also interested in fairness and I want to be sure that you and I are sharing the same information." Don't interrogate or try to corner him or tell him he's being ridiculous. Try not to put him on the defensive. Hold on firmly to your curiosity since it can often elicit important information.

4. SUMMARIZING FREQUENTLY

Sometimes conversations can get bogged down. Everyone feels "stuck," and there seems to be nowhere to go. By summarizing what you have heard from others, you can often release the jam and get things moving again. When you summarize, you give everyone the chance to hear their own statements so they know that you "got it." And, while you are summarizing they can be using the pause in the action to be thoughtful and to reevaluate what they have heard in the room.

You'll want to give "bullet points" of what you've all heard up to this point. Don't try to repeat every little detail—see if you can hit the highlights and get everyone to agree that you have done so by asking, "Did I get everything right?" If you missed something, you'll certainly hear about it and you can graciously add it to the summary in your own words. Ask if you fully understood each person's perspective and, most important, captured all of their interests. Once everyone agrees that the summary is accurate, this often gets the conversation moving forward. It opens the floor to new ideas and can get people thinking about whether they have anything new to contribute.

5. REFRAMING TO TURN DOWN THE HEAT & SHED MORE LIGHT

Things can get pretty intense in family discussions. Sometimes accusations, blame, perceived motives, and insults can take over the conversation. This is when you will need to call upon your most nuanced Active Listening skill: the reframe. In reframing, we introduce a different categorization or perception of a situation or statement. A reframe focuses on interests—in fact, this focus on interests is what reframing is all about. Reframing often turns down the heat by removing judgments and inflammatory statements.

Here's an example:

> Your sister Anne says, *"Arthur is such a micromanager— telling me how to better care for Mom all the time. I'm not his employee, and he can't treat me like his lackey! He has no idea of all I do!"*

> A helpful reframe might be: *"It sounds like you want to be acknowledged for what you do every day for Mom. You'd like to figure out a way for Arthur to understand and appreciate what you do and to trust you more."*

This reframe has gone directly to Anne's interests: She wants acknowledgement, respect, and trust. You nicely side-stepped the insulting comments about Arthur and refocused the conversation onto Anne's interests. Well done.

Reframing takes practice. It requires that you look for the underlying concerns and values that may be driving someone to make a challenging or upsetting statement to you or to others. You will need to be calm, observant, empathetic, and curious in order to consider and introduce alternate perspectives. As you can imagine, this is a skill that requires some courage as well. So try practicing this in your day-to-day conversations—see if you can focus on others' interests and help them to reframe their perspective. Here's another example:

> You are having dinner with your friend. She's telling you a story about how difficult her landlord has become. She goes on a tirade saying: *"He's so greedy and only cares about money! I pay a ton every month—on time, I might add—and he can darn well get himself over here to make sure this dump of an apartment isn't over-run by rats, but he's too cheap and lazy to replace the trash containers! And he never fixed the crack in the window, and now the draft is costing me a fortune in extra heating bills. He has no self-respect! It's not my responsibility to do his job for him. He just thinks I don't notice, but he's gonna be sorry when I call the health board and they fine him."*

> A reframe might look like this: *"Wow, you seem pretty upset with the situation. It sounds like you feel that you hold up your end of the bargain by paying your rent on time and that you want him to keep up his side of the bargain, too. You don't want to incur unnecessary heating costs, and you don't want to get the Board of Health involved, but you need the problems fixed."*

6. USING TECHNOLOGY WISELY

Technology can be a double-edged sword. While it can make communication significantly more efficient, especially when people live far apart, it also can make it more complicated.

How many times have you waited for a response from a sibling who subsequently tells you she never received your email? Or you may know that your brother always carries his cell phone, but it appears that he just screens out any calls from you. And no one in your family seems to know how to receive text messages, let alone respond to them.

Technology is playing an ever-growing role in our communications, but the learning curve is not the same for all of us, especially for the older generation or siblings without children to show them the way. Some of us check email hourly, while others choose to check it weekly. This in itself can be the source of communication problems. Don't assume that the email you sent to all your siblings was adequate for getting the word out about your mother's recent fall. Have a conversation with all family members to determine a workable and reliable system for communicating. And remember: A visit or a phone call will allow your feelings and intentions to be more accurately perceived by others. Emails lack the intonation of the human voice, and your emotions can be missed or misunderstood in written communication. It may seem less efficient to pick up the phone, but it could save you time and stress in the long run.

"But," you say, "my brother and I always argue when we talk to one another. It's better for us to send emails." You may have discovered that you can be more diplomatic when given some time to respond. We call this asynchronous communication, or communication that doesn't occur in "real time" but instead has a built-in time delay. For some families, this works just fine. If this is the case, you may want to use emails for the bulk of your communication, but be aware that an occasional phone call may go a long way towards maintaining or rebuilding the feeling of family.

7. INTRODUCING OPTIMISM TO MOVE THE CONVERSATION FORWARD

When families are in conflict they may begin to lose hope; the future may look pretty bleak. In fact, some siblings may be at the point where they have given up on the possibility of ever resolving the dispute—and important or even critical decisions may be put on hold. When this happens, their parents' safety may be at risk, or they may lose opportunities like accepting an attractive offer on a property, or some family members may miss out on shared holidays or festive family events.

How can you introduce optimism when everyone is feeling frustrated and wrung out? Optimism implies hope, and hope may be just what is needed.

First, you will need to think deeply about how you can bring optimism into such a situation. It's important to stay grounded in reality. Right now, there may be trust issues or anger or fear—and these are obviously barriers to successful collaboration. Acknowledge this, but also ask others to look at what you all may have already achieved together. Maybe you are all sitting together at a family meeting for the first time in years—that's no small feat. This meeting alone is a great sign of group determination, and everyone should be applauded for their efforts. You all got there. Or, if the meeting is by phone for some or all participants, you all still set aside this time. That's an important first step, and it shows that each member of the family is motivated to work toward resolution. This is something to highlight when the conversation stalls. And since you all share the goal of ultimately making some important decisions that are acceptable to everyone, you can remind your family that they are already on the road to creating a "team" or a "board of directors."

Another way to inject optimism is to think about what you have done well together in the past. What previous struggles and successes have you experienced together? Remind them of the time when you all worked together to bail out your neighbor's basement or when you all ran in the 5k race for breast cancer research. And don't forget how you all managed to deal with Uncle Joe when he was asking everybody for money at your cousin Sarah's wedding. While you may be struggling to see eye to eye today, you may have some shared memories of how you worked well as a family in the past. Talk about these "old times" and see if others agree that you still have the skills to work as a team.

To keep everyone motivated, it can also be helpful to remind your family members of their common interests—which might include fairness, Mom and Dad's financial security, or Mom's health. Recognizing these can be a critical first step. Maybe you all have agreed that you need to come up with a better plan for working together on future decisions. You all want things to be less stressful. These common interests can be a great source of encouragement when the discussion gets bogged down.

Remember that when you are providing optimism you don't want to overdo it, as others may view you as a Pollyanna. You also want to make sure the timing is right. And, most importantly, be authentic; others will feel patronized if your words ring hollow.

If, after some exhausting hours of conversation, you sense frustration among your family members about their inability to reach full resolution concerning all the issues on the table, remind them of the progress you all have made. Maybe you have all already agreed that Louise needs some sort of help taking care of Dad. Maybe you have agreed to set up an online calendar for the family to use in managing Dad's needs. This progress can be acknowledged and used as a way to encourage optimism that the thornier details can be addressed successfully as well.

8. USING TRANSPARENCY TO BUILD TRUST

While you may be truly ready to put aside your own position in an effort to help your family reach consensus, you may be worried that others will distrust your motives or doubt your sincerity. Despite your good intentions, they may indeed have some distrust, and it may be difficult for you to act as the family "mediator" if you have not been seen in this role in the past. Your family members may wonder what's going on with you. In our practice, we find that transparency— or being very open about your own goals, thoughts, and feelings— can be very effective in developing trust when it is followed up with consistent use of Active Listening skills.

You might tell your family that you are concerned about the constant bickering and the stalemate that has left important matters in limbo. You can say that you would like to take on a new role in order to move the conversation forward. You may want to remind them that you are new at this, or let them know when you feel "stuck" or worried about the progress of the discussion. Be open and sincere about any discomfort you might experience. That will show them that you are trying to be helpful and that you could use their support.

While transparency builds trust, it takes time and consistency.

9. USING "AND" INSTEAD OF "BUT"

This is a simple concept that can be a marvelously effective tool. No progress will be made when you say something like: "I understand how that happened, but you should have known that Mom would get upset." "But" is the big eraser—it erases the benefit gained by a statement of understanding. "But" can leave the other person angrier than when you started. It can seem to negate whatever came before it. "And," on the other hand, builds off what was said before. So you might say, "I understand that you were stuck in traffic which was beyond your control" followed by "and I wish you had thought to call me so I could pick up Mom instead of leaving her waiting." That still conveys your displeasure at what was done, and yet doesn't negate the acknowledgement. Try this, you'll find that you are more able to make your point if you think to say "and" in place of "but."

10. AVOIDING TOXIC QUESTIONS AND COMMENTS

Now that you've reviewed some positive Active Listening tools to use, let's look at some common traps that are lurking around the landscape of family conversations. Do you see some "don'ts" below that feel familiar to you?

Let's take a look at some ways for you to avoid making things worse in a difficult conversation. With practice, you can be a role model for your family and your skills are likely to improve the tone of the conversation for everyone.

Don't circulate negative comments.

Instead of: *"Jill, you always say that you're too busy to help out."*

Try: *"Jill, can we look at what tasks you might be able to commit to?"*

Don't attribute motives.

Instead of: *"You just want to move-in with Mom so you can live rent free."*

Try: *"Can we all talk about how you see your role as caregiver* and what that means in terms of your financial arrangements with Mom?"

Don't judge or assign blame.

Instead of: *"You know, we wouldn't be in this mess, Hank, if you hadn't been so careless with money."*

Try: *"I know that the financial situation is upsetting for everyone. Let's see if we can work together to start looking for solutions and considering some new ideas."*

Don't focus on negatives.

Instead of: *"This is hopeless, we never get anywhere with these conversations."*

Try: *"I know that our past conversations have been frustrating for all of us. Can we try a new approach where we agree to listen respectfully to one another? I promise to try <u>my</u> best to do this."*

Don't thoughtlessly follow theories.

Instead of: *"Once she stops driving, she will have to move to a place with more services."*

Try: *"If Mom is no longer driving, we will need to consider how she will get her groceries and go to her doctors' appointments, her hairdresser, and committee meetings. And maybe there are other places that she still drives to, so let's just ask her if there is anything we might not have considered."*

Don't focus on the past.

Instead of: *"You always used the beach house much more than any of us."*

Try: *"Equalizing the use of the house is important to me, and I want to talk about how we can take that into consideration in the future."*

Don't ask leading/solution-oriented questions.

Instead of: *"Dad, don't you think you really need more help around the house now!"*

Try: *"Dad, can we talk about how you want to manage your housekeeping and cooking needs now that you are using a walker in the house?"*

Don't contribute to the conflict by fueling animosities.

Instead of: *"Roger, you've never respected my opinions."*

Try: *"Roger, I hope that we can listen to one another and try to work together on this."*

Family conversations can be fraught with danger. Don't enter the fray unprepared. Set your *GPS* to Active Listening with the goal of encouraging others to think about and share their underlying interests. Note that in this mode your *GPS* is not just focused on the destination. It's giving great weight to how you get there and what alternate routes may exist. Ignite your own curiosity in order to become a careful and authentic questioner and listener. Remember that your Active Listening kit has many tools and you can select those that fit your situation best. Be brave and be transparent.

———

Active Listening requires a set of skills that may be challenging for you, especially when you're upset and frustrated. Begin using the skills that come most easily to you and incorporate the others as you can. You will be surprised how, when you help someone to feel heard, they become better at hearing you. Once you both feel listened to, a more productive dialogue will follow.

4

....

MOVING FROM INTERESTS TO OPTIONS

Realtors say, *"Location, Location, Location!"* Mediators preach, *"Interests, Interests, and Interests!"* But what you are probably thinking is, *"What's really important to me is just getting to Solution, Agreement, Finality!"*

You probably are reading this guide in the hope that one day soon you will wake up and find that all the stress of your particular family feud is behind you—finally resolved, done, history. Life can begin anew for your family, and you can move on.

It can be helpful to remember that sometimes, in order to get to our destination, we need to *"slow down to move fast."*

DON'T SEEK OPTIONS UNTIL
INTERESTS ARE FULLY EXPLORED

It bears repeating that you can't create a well-structured agreement with your family on any matter if you haven't first determined everyone's interests. Although, in the end, your family's resolution may not equally address all the expressed interests, it is critical to understand and acknowledge each of them. A successful outcome can best be achieved when you work together to prioritize interests and to look for creative and perhaps unexplored ways to address these interests. We'll talk more about prioritizing just ahead.

If your family has been talking with Dad about the possibility of moving to the new assisted living facility in town, there could be conflict at the solution level: to move or not to move. But once interests are explored, the conversation can become far richer and offer greater opportunities for creative problem solving. Maybe you think Dad needs to move because he is not eating well and he has not been very compliant with taking his medications. You believe he needs daily supervision. Dad refuses to leave his home because he enjoys his privacy and the familiarity of his surroundings—and moving feels like an overwhelming process. He also has his bird feeders in his yard that he enjoys so much. Your brother Aaron wants Dad to stay at home because he wants to honor Dad's wishes, and he also likes to stay with Dad when he visits from Cleveland. Once all these and other interests are fully explored, it may be possible to do some information gathering and come up with a plan that can meet many or most of them.

BRAINSTORM OPTIONS

You probably already know about brainstorming—everybody throws out ideas in an effort to come up with a plan that is likely to be more successful than any one person would create on their own. It just makes sense to draw from others' knowledge and experience.

In our practice, when we ask families to brainstorm, we encourage them to use a technique known as **Blue Skying.** Here everyone is asked to come up with ideas, any ideas, which would address the interests that have been expressed. They are asked to set aside judgment and leave the bounds of reality. They are encouraged to suggest options <u>as if anything were possible.</u>

Try this, and be sure that someone is recording all the ideas on a flipchart or a large pad of paper. Remember, you will all be aware that everyone's ideas are being listed not because they are necessarily achievable in the real world but because they may have elements that stimulate new thoughts and reveal more about what would be "great" if there were no boundaries or limitations or obstacles (like finances, time, health issues, etc.).

When you Blue Sky a solution, everyone promises not to criticize others' ideas at this stage, and you all strive to be as creative as possible, trying to meet the interests you have already identified.

YOUR FAMILY'S BLUE SKY LIST MIGHT LOOK LIKE THIS:

(You won't attribute names to the list, but we have done so in order to give you an idea of who suggested each Blue Sky option.)

- *(Dad)* Move Dad to the Ritz Carlton where he can get room service for every meal.
- *(Aaron)* Have a caterer deliver hot meals three times a day.
- *(Dad)* Have a full time cook for Dad at home.
- *(Aaron)* Have a nurse drop by twice a day to administer meds.
- *(You)* Get Dad a corner room with bird feeders at the windows in an assisted living community.
- *(You)* Offer to have Aaron stay with you when he is in town—and give him your car to use while he is here.
- *(Dad)* Find a really nice apartment in an over-55 community (with lots of friendly ladies!).
- *(You)* Have all Dad's favorite furniture and collectibles moved to his new place.
- *(You)* Hire a moving service that specializes in elder relocation—to help Dad sort through his unwanted stuff, sell the valuables at auction, and manage a tag sale for the remaining items.

This list could go on and on. Encourage everyone to keep brainstorming until you've all run out of ideas.

CONSIDERING AND EVALUATING YOUR OPTIONS

Now it's time to talk about what might work, what information or research is needed, and what next steps you might want to take. We promised that your *GPS* would **G**uide you from **P**ositions to **S**olutions, but before you can work out a mutually agreed upon plan, you need to look at all the options and figure out which ones might work, what interests they meet, what benefits each option might offer, and what risks they would each involve. Remember that every option should be evaluated in relation to the interests expressed, particularly the common interests like Dad's safety and his emotional well-being. If an option is not realistic (like a room at the Ritz), you can all enjoy a laugh together and then pull out the meaning in the option: Dad would be in a pleasant environment, he would have his nutritional needs met, and he would be "treated like a king." Can some of these benefits be provided via a different option?

From the list that you all created, it seems that you are all genuinely concerned about Dad's happiness, his nutrition, and the proper administering of his daily medications. So this would be the time to start the discussion about priorities. Which interests are most important and why?

In fully exploring interests, we often need to come up with a way to rank or prioritize them. Sometimes it's not possible to find options that satisfy all the interests that have been expressed, so it's helpful to have a good sense of what matters most. It's easy to think of a ranking by number, but an effort to agree upon an order of importance could create another conflict. Sometimes it works better to categorize interests into baskets like: "must haves," "nice to haves," "not necessary." etc. Or: "critical," "really important," "somewhat important," "not important." Simply naming the baskets (categories) can be a good team-building task. It's also a good way of getting everyone invested in the process. Once the baskets are established, you will ask all participants to share their thoughts as to why, for them, specific interests should be put into one basket versus another.

Regarding your father's living situation, you might feel that support for Dad in taking his medications regularly is *critical* and that his remaining in familiar surrounding is *not important*. Your father might feel that remaining in familiar surroundings is *really important* but that his privacy is *critical*. Clearly, this method of addressing priorities can open up deeper communication about values.

You may not agree with your brother's idea about which basket a specific interest should be placed in, but how he feels about it is his reality. So, how might you resolve this difference? What would that conversation look like? Hopefully you would use your Active Listening skills to explore why your brother believes that, for example, it is *really important* that he stay with Dad when he visits. Don't try to change the way he feels; just focus on exploring what his concerns, his desires, his values are. And you can articulate what yours are. This process can sometimes reveal even deeper interests, like Aaron's desire for some quiet quality time with Dad. It turns out that he and Dad have a habit of enjoying early morning conversations over coffee and the morning papers, and Aaron finds that that's when they most connect. So now "quality time together" might be an interest that everyone agrees is *really important*—and this newly revealed interest may even prompt the generation of new options.

Ultimately you will need to decide how you are going to make your decisions. What will an "acceptable" plan look like? Will it have to satisfy all concerns, or those in the *critical* and the *really important* baskets, or just those in the *critical* basket. You get the idea.

Dad has been clear that he really wants to stay in his familiar surroundings, and he has also tossed out some options that would meet your concern about his physical well-being. So he might be ready to talk about how he could balance his desire to stay in his home with his need to be medically safe.

Would he really consider getting some help with meals and with his meds? If so, you would be happy to explore the services available in his community. You might discover that he can have frozen pre-cooked meals delivered from the grocery store along with simple ingredients like sliced cold cuts, peanut butter, whole-wheat crackers, fresh fruit, and apple juice. You would be willing to shop the aisles of the store and create a shopping list that could serve as an order form for his weekly needs. You might find that you could place the order online every Sunday night from your home. And maybe Meals on Wheels could provide some of his meals as well; you could offer to call the regional Area Agency on Aging to find out. As for his medications, Aaron might offer to explore the new electronic dispensing machines that sound an alert when it's time to take a pill.

One way of determining the range of solutions which might ultimately be agreeable to all is to look at your family's **Zone of Possible Agreement** (ZOPA). Simply put, this is your playing field. The boundaries of the field are set by all the parties in the negotiation. If, after fully considering all the interests at play, you determine that you are willing to accept an arrangement where Dad remains at home as long as his health and safety needs are met, then you have proposed boundaries of the playing field that include this possibility along with the possibility that he relocate. If, however, either Aaron or Dad is unwilling to consider moving Dad from his home under any circumstances, then the boundaries are moved inward to create a smaller field of negotiation which does not include relocation. Once the non-negotiables are established, you are left with a Zone of Possible Agreement, where there is overlap for everyone and the details of an agreement can be worked out.

YOUR TIME LINE FOR REACHING AGREEMENT

When confronting a complex and long-standing dispute, your family is unlikely to reach a final agreement in one or two conversations. Even when interests and options have been fully fleshed out, creating solutions often means agreeing to do some homework and setting a timetable for reporting back. And then, once a plan is in place, it is important to make an agreement about when and how to reassess.

Furthermore, time changes everything, and you always want to be ready to make future modifications to your resolution if needed. Maybe Dad will be comfortable and safe at home for several years, but you all may need to look at options again if his health declines at some time in the future. Family disputes are often the result of transition issues, and today's resolution may need to be reconsidered again and again as the years go by.

———

Moving from interests to options takes skill and patience. In order to create a mutually agreed upon resolution that will work well for you and your family, you must be willing to take the time to work through all the possible options before arriving at an agreement. As a family, the ability to make decisions together is an ongoing need, and a good decision-making process will serve you well as future issues arise. In Chapter 12, we will discuss how you can move from options to resolutions that are acceptable to everyone using a clear and effective decision-making system.

5

....

WHY WE GET STUCK:
COMMON BARRIERS TO OVERCOME

W hen you think about it, the real miracle of family life is that we are *ever* able to resolve a major family transition. Many barriers exist that keep us from having productive conversations. While these may indeed be problematic, they are not insurmountable.

Identifying the obstacles is half the battle. Don't despair and fall into the negativity trap as you read through this chapter. It is a long list:

1. Lack of Trust
2. Different Perceptions of Fairness
3. Multiple Issues
4. Poor Communication
5. Geographic Dispersions
6. Entrenched Patterns
7. Current Family Relationships
8. Wealth Disparities
9. Styles of Dealing with Conflict
10. Personality Changes
11. Complicated Role Reversals
12. Passivity
13. Relying on Faulty Assumptions
14. Historical Impasses
15. Emotional Triggers and their Responses

To complement your *GPS* and to help you craft your own success, we will give you suggestions for action steps for each of these barriers. Let's take them one at a time.

BARRIER 1: Lack of Trust

Trust is difficult to define, but you know when it's there and when it's not. So what is it? Trust is the perception that others are being honest and genuinely engaged, and a belief that they have integrity and will follow through on their commitments.

Trust may have been lost among family members over the years, and collaboration can seem impossible without the foundation of trust. Rebuilding trust is a slow process since it must be tested over time. So what can you do when immediate planning is essential?

Possible solution:

When trust is missing, other assurances must be built into agreements. You will need to face the "what-ifs" squarely from the beginning so everyone knows how commitments will be secured.

For example, if you fear that your sister is likely to "forget" about your Dad's doctor's appointment next month, you might suggest that a system be in place to provide you with the needed security. Maybe you will ask her to email you the night before the appointment to let you know that she will be there as planned. As part of the plan, you will both agree that, if you don't receive an email, you will call her cell phone at 7AM that morning to remind her. If you think that she will be offended by this plan, try framing it in terms of your interests.

Your side of the conversation might sound something like this:
"Francine, I am grateful that you are going to take Dad to see Dr. Merkin next month. This will be a great help to me with my tight work schedule. I do worry, however, that you are also very busy. Would you mind letting me know on the night before that all is well and you are planning to pick Dad up for the appointment? If we don't connect, I'll give you a call early the next morning. This would give me a great deal of comfort."

BARRIER 2: Different Perceptions of Fairness

Another barrier that frequently obstructs the road from conflict to collaboration is different perceptions of fairness. This is one of the most common reasons why families get stuck. Everyone brings his or her own definition of fairness, and any situation that doesn't meet a person's construct is deemed unfair, and hence unacceptable.

So if Mom and Dad gave everyone a down payment for their first house, and you moved into your spouse's house and thus needed no down payment, you might now think you should get some additional compensation when distributing property. Similarly, if your parents paid college tuition for all their grandchildren and your brother Bobby had no children, he may feel short changed. Whether or not he "should" feel short changed or you "should" be entitled to some additional compensation is a matter of perception. Regardless of who is "right," feelings of inequity can fuel conflict and set up high barriers to resolution.

"Fair" can be a four-letter-word when it is used without clarity as to what it means to each person in the room. Does it mean "equal"— giving the same dollar amount to each person? Or "equitable"— taking into account differences between you all in your needs, your standing in the family, and what you have contributed over the years? While fairness may be expressed as an interest on its own, it can also be a bucket containing one or more other interests, such as a desire for love, recognition, or appreciation by family members.

Possible solution:

When you hear, *"I just don't think that's fair,"* your follow-up should be directed towards uncovering underlying interests. Use your Active Listening skills to explore what lies beneath the statement. It may be helpful to ask your "aggrieved" brother to explain what he thinks would make the situation "fair." What do others believe your parents intended? How can their intention be better understood? Showing you hear how and why your brother thinks he should get some recompense can go a long way to coming up with a workable solution.

It can also be helpful if you all talk about the many faces of "fairness." Listen to each other's definitions and work with one another to create a mutually acceptable definition. As with any value we hold dear (like honesty, kindness, etc.), the pursuit of fairness can create ethical dilemmas with which we must grapple as individuals and as families. Fairness can be viewed broadly or in a very narrow way. It can look to the past, the present, and the future.

So, if Bobby thinks it's unfair that his siblings each benefited from Mom and Dad's contributions to college expenses for their kids, he might take a different view if the conversation were framed as a discussion about how his *nieces and nephews* benefitted from their *grandparents'* generosity. He might rethink how he measures fairness if your discussion included the possibility that your parents may have wished to distribute their estate to all of their heirs, not just to their children.

And, as for your own request for compensation to balance the amount of the down payments received by your siblings, you might reconsider your position if your view of fairness were broadened from "equal" to "equitable" to also include "need."

In the end, it is still up to each person to determine for themselves what feels fair; considering various definitions and viewpoints, and looking for creative ways to meet the underlying interests revealed, can broaden the possibilities for everyone.

BARRIER 3: Multiple Issues

Unfortunately, there's rarely just one simple issue that you as a family need to confront.

Let's look at another example. Maybe the presenting problem seems to be Dad's driving and whether or not to "take away his car keys"— he refuses to even talk about it. But what about those burned pots in his kitchen and his increasing forgetfulness and dramatic mood swings? What about his depression and your suspicion that it's caused by all the pressure he is under from his blended family? You and your siblings simply don't get along with his second wife's kids.

To make matters more complicated, you know that Dad didn't instantly become a really bad driver or begin to burn every meal. It's been a slow process of decline. When does driving or cooking cross the line from being an appropriate activity to being a dangerous one?

Finally, there is the whole finances thing. He used to be on a budget and that completely flew out the window with his second wife. She finds those TV shopping networks irresistible and, from her wheelchair, she manages to spend like a drunken sailor. And you worry that he's beginning to pay some bills twice or not at all. What a mess. How can you begin to work through this morass?

Possible solution:

Pick your battles strategically. Remember the old saying that "a trip of a thousand miles begins with a single step." But don't forget that which direction you take is just as important as moving that first foot.

If there's not an immediate crisis or serious safety concern, begin by addressing the issues that will raise the least amount of conflict, the proverbial low hanging fruit. Maybe you could talk to Dad about his housekeeping and cooking needs and see if you could ask your siblings to work with you in hiring some household help. Once that is managed, celebrate the agreement before moving on to the more contentious discussions around finances or driving concerns.

And when safety is seriously at issue or when a crisis seems imminent, or when you are concerned about possible abuse or neglect, address the issues first that are of most immediate concern.

BARRIER 4: Poor Communication

Even when your family is not under stress, you know your family communication is not optimal. Patterns of who talks to whom seem set in stone. You call Mom on Sundays, but your sister June talks to her every day. Your brother Ned barely ever speaks with either of them, or with your other sister Ruth Ann, so he depends on you to keep him in the loop.

Beyond these patterns, styles of communication can also vary in a family, and they probably do in yours. Note that there are many ways to categorize communication styles. One way is to consider a four-style model. In this model, people tend to fall within a spectrum of being assertive, aggressive, passive, or passive-aggressive. Not surprisingly, most people don't label their own style as being aggressive, and the strength of this style will vary depending on the particular issues at hand. Even if someone appears aggressive, they may not be aware of how they are perceived or how they make others feel.

For example, Bill doesn't know he is perceived as dominating in his family interactions. To him, he is just being "normal," the way he always is. His sister, however, feels intimidated and becomes passive so as not to ruffle his feathers. To complicate these interactions, communication styles may become exaggerated when people are under stress.

Often, the most challenging style to deal with is the passive-aggressive style. This behavior can manifest itself in any number of covert ways, from forgetfulness, to ambiguity, to obstruction. The person with passive-aggressive behaviors is a master at subterfuge and can even be completely oblivious to his or her style. If your brother "doesn't remember" to attend the Friday dinner at your house or he promises to get back to you about his availability over Christmas weekend (and never does), he is avoiding direct confrontation but obstructing your plans at every turn. This person's feelings may be so repressed that they don't even realize they are deeply troubled with an issue.

Possible solutions:

One suggestion that can work is to have a discussion about sensitive issues with your closest sibling(s) to strategize about how best to approach the situation. We are not suggesting that you do this in order to gang up on a particularly difficult sibling or parent but rather to do some planning to help smooth the discussion and change the tone of future meetings. We mediators use this technique in our conflict coaching practice when it's not possible to get all the important parties into a room together. We help our coaching clients become more effective listeners, reframers, and collaborative decision makers, and to build on the strengths that already exist in a family. Your brother Steve can say exactly the same thing to your sister Alice as you do, but he gets a smile instead of a frown. She always trusted him more, so use that as a positive force.

And don't forget to use some of the Active Listening skills you learned about in Chapter 3. When dealing with family members whose communication style is creating a barrier to successful team building, be sure to listen more, and to acknowledge, summarize, and empathize. This can really work. Remember to be careful not to appear to be patronizing or artificial. While a neutral mediator can use these skills freely, a radical change in your behavior could make others suspect your motives. If you have never been a good listener before (especially with your brother Frank), you may have to take it slowly and introduce these skills over time. We'll talk more about communication in Chapter 11.

BARRIER 5: Geographic Dispersion

Lack of regular sibling contact might explain John's need to cover his guilt about rarely seeing Mom by bossing the rest of you around whenever he swoops into town. We use the word "swoop" advisedly. John is normally out of sight and out of mind; but now, he is very present. It is an all too common syndrome in the elder world. But who can really blame the "swooper," no matter how annoying. He or she really loves Mom and Dad, and the pent-up need to be of service just pours out—at all the wrong moments.

Unfortunately, guilt isn't the only thing you need to worry about. Geographic dispersion can exacerbate complex processes like issue identification and severity assessment. The sibling without regular contact may be out of touch with the normal subtleties of an elder's changing patterns. The distant sibling may overreact to changes he sees from his last visit with a parent.

Possible solutions:

Think about what responsibilities might be taken on by the out-of-town siblings, like bill paying, web research, or daily check-ins with Dad by phone. The distant siblings do not need to be cut off from caregiving. It may serve everyone's needs if you can find ways for all the siblings to actively participate.

We suggest that you work hard to communicate regularly with all family members. Be sure that everyone is kept in the loop regarding decisions large and small. Again, the web can offer lots of options like blogs and members-only websites such as LotsaHelpingHands.com or OurFamilyWizard.com. And beyond the sibling communication, Mom and Dad would probably be delighted to receive more frequent phone calls. If they are not already using Skype®, they might be ready to learn how to in order to "see" their grandchildren more regularly.

You can have virtual family meetings hosted by a different sibling each time. Or family members might plan a special retreat week-end somewhere between your homes or even somewhere especially enticing (like Key West in the winter). Retreats can provide social time along with work, and distant siblings are not then shouldering all the costs and inconvenience of travel every time there is a family gathering.

BARRIER 6: Entrenched Patterns

You may notice that when you do manage to get everyone in the family into the same room at the same time, your siblings uncon-sciously sit in the spot they were assigned to for dinner 40 or 50 years ago—and revert to the way they behaved then, too. Sally reads emails on her iPhone just like in the old days when she had a book stuffed in her face for protection. Doug, the alpha dog, strolls in late seemingly just to make an entrance, and Mary quietly cries at the slightest sign of conflict. Larry, who might be the least "capable" of your sibs, is also the oldest—which in your traditional parents' eyes trumps everything. So he was made executor and, most annoyingly, starts sitting at the head of the table, carefully eyeing Doug.

To complicate matters further, you have other layers of ancient entrenched patterns—your family's myths and superstitions. Things like, "Talking about money subverts parental authority," or "Writing a will and doing end-of-life planning will hasten my death." And let's not forget closely held prejudices, like "Mom's definition of maturity is 10 years older than whatever age you are today." These are all powerful notions that you must root out and confront to successfully engage your family. No mean task.

Possible solutions:

Be transparent about everyone's tendency to revert to old roles. Do it with a light touch. Think about empowering younger siblings to take on information-gathering roles or to monitor speaking time as a way of changing patterns in non-threatening ways that will support decision-making. Name the myths and superstitions that thwarted the family in the past—sharing a laugh about your Dad's fear that writing a will would somehow hasten his death, even though he was a doctor and knew better.

BARRIER 7: Current Family Relationships

There are always ongoing relationship issues that manifest themselves most strongly when things get tense. You know that no matter where you start your discussion, Jess will need to somehow insert that Mom always liked Robbie best. Scott has never been able to talk to Kelly, and he'll immediately begin to bicker with her. You can quickly draw up your own family list of dysfunctional "normal" behaviors.

Possible solution:

Have realistic expectations about what is reasonably achievable in your family setting. Simply declaring that everyone should hold hands and begin singing "Kumbaya" won't miraculously change your family into a group of cooperative souls. So don't try any activity that risks ridicule. Relationships have developed over the years for a lot of "good" reasons where "good" means powerful, not wonderful.

If you are instituting several other "barrier solutions" suggested in this guide, you may be surprised how the really problematic family relationship issues can recede into the background when an effective meeting and decision structure has been put into place.

BARRIER 8: Wealth Disparities

Differences in financial circumstances suddenly become germane when financial issues begin to impact decisions. Often a discussion about a property becomes the catalyst for raising the topic of wealth disparities. You may be talking about what to do with the house in Lake Tahoe in light of the fact that sibling use of it is unequal. It is a rare family where all the siblings have the discretionary money to pay for an equal ownership share of an expensive property.

Remember that wealth disparities can create power imbalances. Even when a person of means tries to not exercise his or her financial advantages in the family, that person's opinion and vote might have extra weight in financial discussions.

Possible solutions:

Being gently transparent about these differences and how they seem to impact family decision-making can be uncomfortable at first, but can help in the long run. And you may find that issues that have a wealth dimension can actually be dealt in a forward-looking and creative manner. Dave may be happy to pay proportionately more of the expenses on the summer place. Jane may be able to finance placing a property in a real-estate trust and funding its ongoing maintenance so that she and her siblings enjoy equal access during their lifetimes, with Jane and her estate ultimately owning all of the property in the end. There are many creative ways to cut the wealth pie if family members are imaginative and not defensive.

And remember that legal and financial advice is often essential when taxes, trusts, and other financial matters are in play. Be sure to only include advisors who are acceptable to everyone in the family and who do not have any conflicts of interest.

BARRIER 9: Styles of Dealing with Conflict

Conflict styles are different from communication styles. You might have noticed that, when in conflict, Lynn tends to be an "avoider," Mark is too "accommodating," and Jordan is always "competing" in her dealings with family members. (See the *Thomas-Kilmann Conflict Mode Instrument,* or *TKI,* for a closer look at these styles.) Your challenge is to try to create an environment and process that helps your family to become willing to "collaborate" and "compromise."

Possible solutions:

Don't vilify your most "difficult" siblings. Jordan may really not know that others read her as competitive even when she thinks she is being a softy. You probably won't change her, just work to understand her and try to focus on the content of her proposals rather than her delivery. If others are avoiding conflict or are adding a competitive edge to every discussion, your job will be to provide some balance and to keep the conversation directed toward mutual interests and common goals. When these shared purposes are highlighted, others may be more willing to come around to the team approach that will lead to successful decision-making.

BARRIER 10: Personality Changes

There are a variety of personality changes that can occur with advancing age, illness, and all forms of dementia. Whether it is conflict aversion, paranoia, or an increasing gentleness, each evolves on a continuum of impact that makes action points hard to determine. Maybe Mom has always been the rock of the family, the "go to person" for any issue, but now she simply agrees with each person she talks to because she can't handle conflict the way she used to. This change happened imperceptibly over a couple of decades. Or Dad, to everyone's surprise, is now able to handle the freewheeling lifestyles of his grandchildren in ways he never could with you and your siblings. Drives you crazy, doesn't it?

And don't just focus here on the elders in your family; there may be sibling personality changes to consider, too. Your siblings have also aged and survived their own life events—illnesses, divorces, troubled teenaged children, and so on. They may have developed a more wise and reasoned outlook than they once had, or they may have acquired coping disorders that interfere with their ability to manage new stresses. Too often alcohol and drugs are the elephants in the room. And, your baby sister may be ready to collect social security now. Even lifestyles change over the years: The raging hippie may now be a conservative lawyer.

Along with personality changes, unexpected bursts of emotions can influence family communication—*"I never knew I cared so much about that house until we started talking about selling it."* This syndrome can hit anybody at any time when discussing major family life changes, and the sudden strong feelings may impact how you or your family members interact around specific "hot button" issues.

Possible solution:

Think about making accommodations to maximize the ability of all family members to participate, not just the elder. For example, if your sister has a drinking problem, schedule meetings at times of day when she's most likely to be clear-thinking. Strategies for including the elder's voice—despite any difficult personality changes— are discussed more in Chapter 9.

BARRIER 11: Complicated Role Reversals

We often hear a simplistic mantra about elder transitions, "parents becoming children and children becoming parents," but this just isn't how it works. In fact, it's a downright dangerous assertion. You will never become your parent's parent. You may be changing roles and positions of power, but your parents will never be your children. You may be an adult child driving a parent, or shopping or cooking for them, but your role as a caregiver now is very different from the responsibilities your parents held when you were growing up. All their wisdom and accumulated life experience is still there in some form and should be honored and valued.

Possible solution:

Ultimately, the underlying concern is addressing with respect your parents' vulnerabilities as declining health impacts more and more parts of their lives. Yes, you are doing more for them, but remember to preserve the rituals that show their honored position in the family. Seek their opinions. Maintain their sense of decorum during family meals when they are present, even if the extra bit of formality may not be the norm in your life. You will all be richer for it. Remember that there is a high probability that your children will treat you the same way you treated your parents. So model good behavior.

BARRIER 12: Passivity

Sometimes people who are overwhelmed with multiple issues do nothing—we might call this a "deer in the headlights" mentality, but this is another example of the danger of using a simplistic metaphor in the elder field. Headlights imply you can actually see something that may be a threat. Rather, in complex family situations, there is usually a "web" of concerns and threats. Delicate but strong strands of multiple issues envelop the whole family, and it's hard to see the danger of inaction. Since there is no simple solution in sight, this complexity too often translates into no action at all. Where do you start? Determining what issue to deal with in an actionable way can seem like an impossible maze to navigate.

When faced with an unpleasant situation, some of us wrap ourselves in the warm blanket of denial. It may not offer much protection from a storm, but it feels good enough for now. And many of us would prefer to keep things the way they are for as long as possible. Change means risk. Things could always be worse. So we resist change even when we suspect that change might make life better in the long run. And we put off conversations in which we would be asked to even discuss major changes.

Passivity can be brought on by denial or inertia or fear of the unknown, or (let's admit it) an unwillingness to manage the overwhelming tasks that may accompany additional caregiving responsibilities or the transition to a new home. With this in mind, it's easy to see why families defer difficult conversations that could impact their parents' lives or their own. So nothing gets done. Important decisions are put off and—unfortunately—as time goes by, fewer desirable options may be available as needs become greater.

Possible solutions:

When passivity is an obstacle to reasoned decision-making, it's helpful to use your *GPS* to find out if there is more information needed or if various assumptions are getting in the way. Try asking what assumptions are at play (*"I can't possibly deal with cleaning out this old house and getting it ready to sell"*). Once the fears are on the table (such as the time and effort needed to empty the house, the back and forth interaction with realtors, the worry about how to know what price to accept for the property, and so on), it is possible to carve up these tasks and find a way to manage them all on a workable schedule.

And don't underestimate the fear of change. Acknowledging this fear for yourself, and using your Active Listening skills to acknowledge it for others, can help loosen fear's grip on you all. Yes, change can be scary. And it can also bring up feelings of loss that may need to be acknowledged and grieved. But it can also open new opportunities when addressed thoughtfully and with a concern for everyone's interests.

Sometimes agreeing on the need for a change can be the hardest part. Whether a change is big or small, most anything can be accomplished if it is taken in bite-sized pieces over a long enough period of time. This is where the family can work together and begin to think like a team. Many hands make light work. And passivity can be overcome when the team takes on important responsibilities in mutually agreed upon ways.

BARRIER 13: Relying on Faulty Assumptions

Our assumptions are the product of less than complete information, and they can often become barriers to progress. They are born when we unconsciously filter this limited information through our past experiences, knowledge, biases, fears, desires, and values. You understand this now that you have your own well engineered *GPS*.

Possible solution:

Remember what you learned back in Chapter 1—think like an investigator! Look at what you and your family members may each have observed, and how you may have filtered your observations and made assumptions. Consider how you can all work together to either verify or debunk these assumptions. Spend some respectful time reviewing each of your observations and assumptions. This will help you all to feel less lost and much further along the road to agreement—and you <u>can</u> get there *as a team*.

Say your mother's brother Sam is coming to visit her. You may assume that he will be asking her for money—*yet again*. It's happened before, and you are ready to call him and let him know that you are *on* to him. But your sister Jan spoke with Sam recently to tell him that Mom would be moving soon, so *she* believes that Sam is headed into town to help your mother sort through the family photos and old mementos in the attic. You don't want Sam anywhere near your mother without supervision, but Jan is thrilled to imagine the two of them reuniting and enjoying their shared memories together.

First, you and Jan could simply compare your observations: She spoke to Sam directly but you heard about his visit from Mom, who gave you no details about the reason for his visit. Then you and Jan could respectfully discuss the assumptions you are both making: You believe that he is coming to pressure your mother to give him another "loan" that he will never repay. Jan has always enjoyed Sam. They were very close when she was growing up, and she always thinks the best of people; she would never suspect anything!

Your conversation with Jan will help you both to explore what you know, what you think you know, and what past experiences or values are influencing your perceptions. And you will be in a good place to consider together what you need to do to confirm or disprove any of the assumptions at play here. Jan might be able to acknowledge that you have good reason to distrust Sam; and you might agree that it is, in fact, possible for his motives to be pure in this situation. Given that neither of you are sure about your assumptions, you could jointly agree on what steps you might take to protect your mother and to avoid unnecessary damage to family relationships. You might agree that Jan would stay with Mom during Sam's visit, or you could simply come into town before Sam arrives to finish closing Mom's checking account and funding her trust, as you and your Mom had already planned.

By working together to examine your assumptions, you can determine how to get missing information and adjust your thinking as needed to avoid missteps.

BARRIER 14: Historical Impasses

When we are having a difficult conversation in which we all have the goal of moving forward and making some important decisions, we may be wasting our limited time together trying to ascertain the "truth" about what happened, trying to get out all the "facts," or trying to lay blame. If we disagree about the past and we are stuck trying to resolve that difference, we can easily get caught up in a struggle that is evidence-based and inconclusive. Remember, it's the future that matters and that is where we should be directing our attention ... moving forward using our *GPS*.

Possible solutions:

Focus on the future. Don't try to figure out who was supposed to arrange for the contractor to come look at the porch. It didn't happen, and it's just one more item on a long list of things to manage. It's always hard making any contractor arrangements for the beach house. So keep moving forward, and try to determine who is willing and able to take on the necessary tasks and what commitments can be made now.

If meeting summaries or written agreements might be helpful to avoid misunderstandings in the future, then begin having someone produce such notes for everyone to see.

BARRIER 15: Emotional Triggers and Poorly Managed Responses

Hopefully, you know your own hot-button issues. And it's likely that you know how to get a rise out of every family member by going after his or her emotional triggers. Maybe you avoid any talk about your son's past drug use, or your sister is still feeling raw about how her first husband bungled every financial investment he made. Often, family members have issues that will set them off. These sensitive topics can cause such negative reactions that they divert the conversation away from effective decision-making and sabotage the potential for a deliberative process for everyone.

Yelling, fist pounding, and door slamming outbursts are real show-stoppers; they can bring any conversation to a halt. Or maybe it's the lack of engagement that derails a negotiation. Like when, after being confronted with allegations of financial mis-management, your brother simply refused to participate in the discussion and now he won't take anyone's phone calls.

You probably can name other "bad behaviors" that were the last straw before the game was called. Someone was dominating the conversation, and you almost never got a chance to speak. Or, they interrupted you again and again, as soon as you took a breath. Or maybe someone started crying, and you couldn't continue making your point. Or your sister, the big-time lawyer, was always spouting off about the law and threatening suit. Or your father, who has no patience with these "tedious conversations," just walked out before you all could make any progress. These behaviors (over-reactions, disengagement, threats, impatience, and so on) can happen to any family at any time. Some are predictable; some seem to come out of nowhere.

Possible solutions:

It's best to avoid hot buttons unless they are absolutely pertinent to the conversation at hand. And if they are, remember that trans-parency (why this sensitive topic needs to be discussed), empathy (expressing that you are attuned to their discomfort), and delicacy (using respectful language and a gentle touch) are required to keep the discussion on track.

Setting basic ground rules for the conversation can keep the con-versation from getting derailed. For example, it can be helpful if everyone agrees in advance to honor one another's right to call foul, or that they will say "ouch" or give some agreed upon signal to indicate that they felt stung by a particular comment. This immediate feedback can give you all the chance to pause briefly—and either deal with the "ouch" or agree to move on—before more damage is done. As always, respect is paramount and staying clear of emotional triggers will benefit everyone.

While serious anger control issues may be beyond our ability to manage, we can often ameliorate frustration in high-conflict situations by empathetically acknowledging it. Simple yet powerful acknowledgments can be helpful in response to any of these behaviors: *"You're frustrated, I know. This is hard." "I can see that you are angry. Let's try to talk this through and see if I can better understand what's going on for you."*

Maybe your family doesn't have angry outbursts, but your brother endlessly repeats himself, and you can see that others are losing patience with him and with the entire conversation. Emotions come in layers, and acknowledgement can work wonders. You may remember this from the Active Listening section of Chapter 3. Sometimes, when people repeat themselves it is because they don't feel heard. So reflecting back to your brother what you just heard him say, asking him if you "got it right," and asking him what you might have missed, may reassure him that you have heard his point of view and enable him to settle back and listen to other views in the room.

———

There are so many potential barriers to successful collaboration! While the possible solutions suggested here may help you overcome these common obstacles, some situations could require significant time, professional help, or additional resources to be resolved. In our next chapter, we'll discuss additional tools and strategies that can work across the board and can help make any negotiation go more smoothly. Even so, remember, if you feel overwhelmed, there are many resources available for you and your family. We've listed some at the end of the book.

6

GENERAL STRATEGIES
FOR ANY BARRIER

In addition to the targeted tools and strategies that we have just discussed, we'd like you to consider each of the following suggestions for use in any difficult conversation.

- Try a Little Humor
- Take a Walk in Her Shoes
- Separate the Person from the Problem
- Remember Optimism
- Break Bread Together
- Consider the Alternative

You'll find that some of these approaches come naturally to you. As always, you should lean on your strengths but try to incorporate some new techniques. You may be surprised to find that it makes a difference and moves the conversation forward.

TRY A LITTLE HUMOR

Properly used, humor can do a bunch of wonderful things. Injecting a little humor into a potentially tense meeting can quickly change the tone and help relieve tension. Humor makes it easier to be tough without offending anybody and can help deliver difficult messages. Humor helps when you don't want to answer a question or you want to change the subject. And best of all, it shows that you don't take yourself too seriously.

Obviously, in a family meeting everyone knows everyone else and hopefully understands the normal family culture around humor. So stay in character. Don't try to artificially inject humor if it's uncomfortable for any reason. Be very mindful: You don't want to use humor to embarrass or demean anyone, and you don't want others to think that you are taking the situation lightly when they feel that the issues at hand are quite serious and urgent.

TAKE A WALK IN HER SHOES

Showing empathy and compassion can make all the difference when you're at impasse. Even if you and your family members can't agree on how to solve a problem, you can express to them your understanding that the situation is difficult, even painful, for them. Family members must be able to listen to and rely on one another. Showing that you care about one another and are emotionally mature enough to convey a sense of shared suffering can be just what is needed to reawaken the dialogue.

SEPARATE THE PERSON FROM THE PROBLEM

Let's state the obvious: Negotiations involve people, and people are not perfect. We tend to see the world from our own point of view. We also are not always the best communicators. And most of us are not particularly good listeners.

In the seminal book *Getting to YES*, Roger Fisher and William Ury outline a number of tools for effective negotiation, one of which is to always "separate the people from the problem." No matter what your relationship, try to sit "on the same side of the table" as you look at any issue, so that you face the problem together. Try to structure the negotiation as a side-by-side activity in which, even with different interests, perceptions, and emotional involvement, you are "building a working relationship" and "facing the problem, not the people." Remember, you all share the goal of wanting to put this dispute in the rearview mirror, and you can only achieve this by working together.

REMEMBER OPTIMISM

Capture each success to create momentum. Let's say you are discussing the sale of that ski lodge in the mountains, and you haven't yet come to an agreement on whether or not to sell it—but you did at least all agree on how to share this winter's weekends. Treat that partial agreement as a success and capture it. *"We have done a lot of good work here today and come to agreement on that always tough issue of ski time allotment!"*

BREAK BREAD TOGETHER

Try to include a meal in your family meeting plan. There may be no better positive break in any difficult action than good food shared. A meal built around classic family recipes can work wonders. Or, if cooking is a source of stress in your family, order take-out from a favorite local restaurant that can satisfy everyone's taste. And don't forget to have snacks and beverages on hand during your meeting. If Mom loves M&Ms® or Bob drinks Coca-Cola® by the gallon, bring these along and don't overlook anyone's preferences, including the celery and carrots that Rebecca finds so appealing.

FINALLY, CONSIDER THE ALTERNATIVE!

When we negotiate, we can easily get wrapped up in our goal of reaching our own predetermined solution. You remember—we call this our "position." If you or anyone else is unwilling to back down from your position, or if you just cannot find an option that you can all live with, you will want to be certain that you have fully considered what alternatives are available to you if your negotiation breaks down.

Away from the table, you will be free to take whatever next steps seem best to you. Hopefully, you know very well what your best alternative is. Maybe it's continuing to provide most of the caregiving for your mother by yourself, even though it seems so overwhelming. Maybe it's asking some neighbors and church members outside the family for occasional help. Maybe it's an expensive and unpredictable lawsuit. And maybe your mother will be furious at you—and your kids will be disappointed in you—if you don't achieve a resolution here with your family instead. So ask yourself if the disappointing option on the table is actually better than your best alternative. If it is, then you should carefully consider what you will be facing if you or someone else gets up and leaves your family's "negotiating table" before you reach resolution.

Your best alternative is your "BATNA" (Best Alternative to a Negotiated Agreement, coined by Fisher and Ury in *Getting to YES* and now a standard negotiation term). It might be an acceptable alternative for you, or it might be something you fervently wish to avoid. If your family just can't come to terms about the future of the Vermont house, you know that you can still try to force the sale in court. If this is your best alternative, you need to weigh it against the proposal that others are currently supporting—that you all continue to share the costs of maintaining the house for two more years. A court battle will, you know, cost tens of thousands of dollars and will fracture your family relationships further. If this is your BATNA, then maybe you will want to agree to something that offers hope of a better result, even if it means waiting two more years before you can get what you really want.

Given everything you know about your family members, you may be able to assess their BATNAs as well. Doing so will enable you to better negotiate with them. Maybe your siblings' BATNA is to do nothing, keep the house, and hope you will pay your share of the monthly expenses. But they know you might stop sending your check and you could even take them to court. Thinking about their possible BATNAs can help you to figure out a way to offer something more appealing to them: *"Keeping the house in the family is important to you, and I would like to come up with a plan to do so without it costing me more than I can afford. How would you feel about excusing me from my monthly obligations for some period of time and reducing my share of the equity proportionately?"* Knowing that they can't make you send your check each month and that they do not want to risk having you force the sale, you are beginning to think about ways to meet everyone's interests and create options that are better than each family member's BATNA.

In family situations particularly, everyone's evaluation of his or her BATNA against the options on the table is likely to include an element that considers ongoing relationships. Knowing how important these relationships are to you and to others in your family can provide you with important information about what is at stake for everyone concerned. If there are cousins or grandchildren in the family, those who are at the table in a dispute will often take into account how the extended family will be impacted by their negotiations. And if the conversation gets off track and you're at an impasse, it may be time to get help from a mediator or neutral facilitator who is trusted by everyone at the table.

The family's history and its future may be at stake, and a failed negotiation could have far reaching consequences.

—•—

Having a large toolbox is important when discussions bog down or fall off the rails. While not all strategies work all the time, those discussed above could help to move the conversation forward. Be mindful of what techniques you are choosing and why—you may be surprised by a new type of response from your family.

7

APOLOGIES

It's a phrase with just two little words, but it can be so complicated—*"I'm sorry."* So hard to say, so hard to accept, and so hard to believe.

"She didn't even say she was sorry. ... "
"He said 'sorry' but I know he didn't really mean it."
"I don't care if he's sorry—it's too late now."

Why is an apology so tough—so difficult to give, and sometimes so difficult to accept? And why do apologies sometimes seem to work magic and make the problem go away?

Apologies come in all different shapes and sizes. They can be long or short, simple or complicated. They can be given for personal gain or be full of genuine emotion, caring, and compassion. Apologies, more than anything else, can rebuild bridges and heal wounds. They can, when delivered appropriately, make all the difference.

They can, however, also fall on deaf ears, ring hollow, or raise suspicion. What makes the difference? How do you know if you should apologize? How do you know if you should accept an apology?

It may sound simplistic, but you need to go with your gut. Usually, you know if you did or said something that hurt another. Whether or not you *meant* it, you know if you caused pain. Similarly, if someone who caused you pain says she's sorry, you can usually tell from the feeling you get if there is truth in what you are hearing. You know if she really means it when she apologizes. Not just because there are tears, and not just because she really was wrong, but maybe because you can see a change in her body language or facial expression, or because she seems to be speaking from the heart.

In essence, for an apology to be effective, the apologizer must take responsibility unconditionally. He/she cannot say, *"I'm sorry BUT if you hadn't...."* Similarly, they cannot explain away the transgression by saying *"I'm sorry it happened although it wasn't my fault because...."*

Furthermore, an apology must satisfy some need of the receiver. For example, it must appropriately deal with blame for the offence in question. As the apologizer, you can either accept the blame and/or make some type of commitment regarding future restitution. Another way to make the apology effective is for you to demonstrate that you too are in pain and are trying to repair the damage done.

Let's say you find yourself in a situation where you know you should apologize: Your sister organized a family dinner party for your mother's birthday, and you said you'd come and bring the salad. But, as fate would have it, you got busy at work. This put you in a bind—you could disappoint your client and/or risk the wrath of your boss by leaving work at 6:30, or you could stay to finish the project and hope to catch the end of the party, if you were lucky. As it turned out, you convinced your assistant to stay to help you get the project done, and you left the office as soon as you could, drove at breakneck speed and—feeling stressed and tired—you arrived in time for dessert. Your sister was furious, and there was a general consensus that you'd dropped the ball *again*, not taking family events seriously enough to make them a priority. It wasn't the first time. What should you do?

You could apologize, but you believe it wasn't totally your fault—the economy is dreadful, and if you don't do everything possible, you could lose your job. You know you said you'd be there, but you're not in control and you did your best. As it was, you cut some corners and left before the final version was printed out. Your sister should thank you for your valiant attempts to get out of the office and make it to the party at all! But no; you're in the dog house, and nobody's happy.

In cases like this, it's difficult to apologize. And you take a risk that your apology won't be accepted no matter what you say. So even if you valiantly ignore all the extenuating circumstances you think help explain your lateness, and you unequivocally say, *"I'm sorry I was so late; I feel terrible,"* you may be rejected with something to the effect of: *"Don't even bother apologizing—you never come through."* You know that the minute you start to defend yourself, the apology will lose its potential positive impact as you negate taking full responsibility.

It's also important to remember that timing is an equally important part of an effective apology process. You must apologize when the receiver is able to choose whether or not to accept your apology. For instance, you should not apologize when the receiver is in a large group and needs to appear to be gracious. Apologies are rarely effective if given in the heat of the moment, when emotions are still high from the precipitating event. While it's important to acknowledge the situation and modestly provide a *mea culpa* as soon as possible, the follow-up, in-depth apology should be reserved for a calm and private moment.

Distinguishing between empathy and apology is critical. Acknowledging emotion is different from apologizing. *"I know you're upset that I'm late"* is empathetic. You are letting your sister know you understand how she feels, but it's not an apology. Showing empathy can work well in many contexts, such as when you are a neutral observer; but when an apology is due, showing empathy can undermine the process. A poor attempt at empathy like *"I know you're angry at me, but it wasn't my fault"* is not an apology. Such a statement shows no acceptance of responsibility, and it will probably just make the situation worse.

Statements masquerading as apologies but deflecting partial responsibility onto the recipient—such as *"I'm sorry you're upset, but who can get to dinner at 7:00 anyway?"*—are even worse. Your sister would doubtless prefer hearing nothing than to be made to feel that it's her fault. She wants to hear an acceptance on your part for at least some portion of the offense—<u>not</u> to hear that she caused the problem and is to blame for your transgression.

For apologies to be effective, the parties must be able to communicate with each other. You need to have the opportunity to explain what happened and acknowledge your role and how sorry you are, and—as mentioned above—the receiver must be able to "hear" what you are saying. The timing must be right for this communication to be possible. If you first show your sister that you have heard her, perhaps by summarizing what she has said, she will be more ready to hear what you have to say. If you say, for example, *"I know I messed up by being late; I didn't even get the salad here in time, let alone come in time to help surprise Mom,"* this will allow your sister to nod her head and say or think *"Yes, you messed up all right."* You will have taken responsibility for the pain you caused. You should not, at this time, defend what you did or explain that it was a terrible time to have dinner. Rather, you should say something like *"I'm sorry I was late—I really didn't mean to be."* This is a very simple acknowledgment that you did something that hurt your sister, and that it was not intentional.

Don't forget: A good apology can be an effective conflict resolution tool. Be sure to use it well, as a poor apology can do more damage than none at all.

8

ABUSE / NEGLECT / SAFETY

The issues of abuse, neglect, and safety are tricky for any family to confront. If there are real concerns in your family, we strongly urge you to go beyond this chapter and seek advice and support from doctors, protective services staff, mental health professionals, clergy, or others who can provide help to you and your family.

The Key Caveat—When considering these topics you must be very careful about "letting things go on as they have in the past because we are family." Please don't allow an abusive or neglectful situation to continue. Act and/ or report.

And if you fear that such action could initially incite further abuse and violence, seek help in creating a safety plan to make changes in a way that reduces the risk of further harm.

Resources are listed on pages 78 and 79.

CONSIDERING WHETHER ELDER ABUSE MAY BE PRESENT

Elder abuse is unfortunately widespread; it occurs in many families— regardless of income, resources, education level, race, or ethnicity. It can also happen in long-term care facilities and in other senior housing settings.

As you think about whether there are issues of elder abuse and neglect in your family, in addition to considering your own observations, check in with your siblings and other family members to see if they have any concerns that should be addressed. Are they worried about Mom or Dad being injured? Have they seen Mom or Dad being yelled at? Are they worried that money may be missing or mishandled? Are they concerned about a parent's safety?

Types of abuse and neglect could include any of the following (see definitions below):

- Physical abuse
- Emotional/psychological abuse
- Sexual abuse
- Healthcare fraud and abuse
- Financial abuse
- Self-neglect
- Caregiver neglect
- Caregiver coercion

Asking some simple questions around these topics and communicating your concerns to each other can help you decide whether to involve a professional.

Here are some general definitions:

PHYSICAL ABUSE—Physical abuse is the use of force that results in physical pain, injury, or impairment. We aren't only talking about physical assaults such as hitting or shoving but also the inappropriate use of restraints or confinement. Inappropriate drug use also falls into this category, as does the withholding of nourishment or medications, and inattention to cleanliness and personal hygiene needs.

EMOTIONAL / PSYCHOLOGICAL ABUSE—This type of abuse can be verbal or nonverbal. In emotional or psychological verbal abuse, people speak in ways that cause emotional distress. This can range from intimidation through yelling and/or threats, to ridicule and humiliation, to regular blaming or scapegoating. It can also include excessive use of profanity.

Nonverbal emotional abuse can be just as powerful as verbal abuse. Examples include ignoring the elder, or isolating the person from friends and favorite activities, or even terrorizing the elder with aggressive or threatening body language.

Emotional abuse can be especially difficult to identify because there are no physical markers; if you have noticed an elder becoming more depressed, anxious, or withdrawn, consider whether emotional abuse may be a possible cause.

SEXUAL ABUSE—Sexual abuse is all about lack of consent. There is a broad range of physical acts that are inappropriate, from showing an elderly person pornographic material; to forcing a person to be present during sex; to not respecting the elder's sense of modesty when bathing, showering, toileting, or changing clothes.

HEALTHCARE FRAUD AND ABUSE—Healthcare abuse, carried out by unethical providers, may include any of the following:

- Charging for care that was deliberately not provided
- Overcharging and/or duplicate billing
- Receiving kickbacks for referrals or for prescribing particular medications, or not prescribing generic drug options when appropriate
- Over-medicating, under-medicating, or providing inadequate care
- Recommending unsound or unnecessary remedies for medical conditions
- Medicare and Medicaid fraud

FINANCIAL ABUSE—At a time when families and elders are struggling with the potential need for elders to give up control of financial matters, they must also be on guard for possible financial abuse. Financial abuse can take many forms.

Things to watch out for are:

- Misuse of an elder's personal checks or credit cards; stealing cash or check deposits; or forging the elder's signature
- Inappropriate refusal to share financial information with the elder
- Unpaid bills
- Charges for unusual products or services
- Unauthorized access to an elder's financial/investment accounts

Also, given the times we live in, everyone must guard against identity theft, fake charities, and any number of varieties of Internet scams.

SELF-NEGLECT—When the elder is living alone and fails to meet his or her own physical, psychological, and/or social needs, this can be self-neglect and must be addressed. Doing so can sometimes be challenging; courts have upheld a person's right to make "bad" decisions, but chronic issues that threaten the viability of a person's life are another matter.

CAREGIVER NEGLECT—This is a complex topic because the needs of an elder can be so complicated and the failure to fulfill a range of caretaking obligations may not be intentional. Is the caregiver overwhelmed and in need of extra help? Or is the caregiver inattentive, unmotivated, or unable to do the job properly? A family member caregiver may honestly believe that the amount of care prescribed is really unnecessary. However, this lack of understanding doesn't make neglect any less serious. The National Center on Elder Abuse reports that over half of the cases of elder mistreatment in home settings involve neglect by caregivers.

CAREGIVER COERCION—The potential for caregiver coercion is very real and families should be alert to this possibility, particularly when a family dispute involves a caregiver. Caregivers are in a very powerful position in the life of an elder. The services they provide are often hidden from scrutiny so their power can sadly be used as a tool to gain compliance in any number of arenas.

RISK FACTORS AMONG CAREGIVERS

Many caregivers—whether they are family members, friends, or professionals—find taking care of an elder to be satisfying and engrossing work. But the demands of elder caregiving can also be extremely stressful. Some of this stress is due to the knowledge that there is only one general direction for care to go—ever escalating as the elder's condition deteriorates. It is only the rate of change that varies. Every family member needs to recognize that the stress of providing care can impact the mental and physical health of the caregiver. Caregiver burnout is common, and it is essential to be aware of the needs of those who are on the front lines of caregiving for our elders.

In many cases, elder abuse, though real, is unintentional. Caregivers pushed beyond their capacities may not mean to lose patience, strike, or ignore the needs of the elder they are caring for. Caregiver depression and substance abuse can also trigger or exacerbate abusive behaviors.

Helping the caregivers in your family to feel supported and to receive the self-care they need may be the best protection you have for avoiding elder abuse, neglect, and safety issues.

THE ELDER'S PROFILE—THE POTENTIAL FOR VICTIMHOOD

While there is no excuse for abuse, some elders are easier to interact with and care for than others. Here are some factors concerning elders themselves that may influence whether they are at greater risk for abuse:

- The intensity of an elder's illnesses and/or dementia. How is his or her personality evolving?
- Is the elder exhibiting aggressive verbal or physical behavior that may be difficult for the caregiver?
- Did the elder have a role as an abusive parent or spouse, or was there a history of domestic violence in the home?
- How do the people involved react to social isolation? Are the elder and caregiver alone together too much of the time?

Again, these factors may influence whether elders are at greater risk for abuse; nothing justifies abuse, and the presence of these risk factors can signal that it may be time to seek preventative professional help.

WHAT ARE THE SIGNS AND SYMPTOMS OF ELDER ABUSE?

Many of the signs and symptoms of elder abuse are the same as symptoms of mental and physical deterioration, so it is important to be aware of the full range of possible causes.

The following are some warning signs of possible elder abuse. If you suspect elder abuse but aren't sure, pay attention to the number of issues that look suspicious. Abuse, when it is occurring, generally has more than one manifestation.

- Frequent arguments or tension between the caregiver and the elderly person
- Changes in personality or behavior in the elder, such as increased depression, anxiety, and withdrawal from communication

- Unexplained signs of injury such as bruises, burns, welts, scars, broken bones, sprains, or dislocations
- Report of drug overdose
- Failure to take medication regularly
- Broken eyeglasses or frames
- Signs of being restrained, such as rope marks on wrists
- Caregiver's refusal to allow you to see the elder alone
- Broken or missing belongings
- Threats to harm pets
- Noticeable weight loss or dehydration
- Lack of proper medical treatment
- Development of skin conditions such as bed sores
- Frequent falls, which while unintentional, may be a sign of neglect
- Unsanitary living conditions
- Inattention to personal hygiene
- Inappropriate clothing for the weather
- Unsafe or hazardous living conditions
- Desertion of or "losing" the elder in a public place
- Caregiver withholding or reading the elder's mail
- Caregiver intentionally obstructing the elder's religious observances, dietary restrictions, holiday participation, visits by minister/priest/rabbi, etc.
- Lack of privacy such as the removal of all doors from the elder's living spaces

Since an elder may be silent about the abuse she or he is experiencing, if you observe these or other signs that concern you, explore what is going on, and seek help if you suspect an elder is in need.

REPORTING ELDER ABUSE

In most states, the first agency to turn to is **Adult Protective Services** (**APS**). Every state has at least one toll-free elder abuse hotline or helpline for reporting elder abuse. See state listings at **www.NCEA.aoa.gov, the National Center on Elder Abuse**. In addition, information and referrals are also available from the national **Eldercare Locator: 1-800-677-1116 or www.eldercare.gov.**

OTHER ISSUES OF ABUSE IN THE FAMILY

While these pages have specifically focused on elder abuse, we recognize that other family members may also be victims of abuse and encourage you to seek help in any case where an individual's safety or well-being may be at risk. A helpful resource for support and safety planning is **The National Domestic Violence Hotline: 1–800–799–SAFE (7233), www.thehotline.org.**

EMERGENCY HELP

If an elder or any individual is in immediate danger, **call 911** or the local **police department** for immediate help.

We have discussed some difficult subjects here; let's hope they don't apply to you and your family in a serious way. If they do, take action now; there is lots of help available. And even if you think they don't, take the opportunity to see if there might be issues in your family's life where you aren't yet in the danger range of abuse or neglect but you see warning signs that could signal potential problems down the line if your family continues on its current path. Getting help now to prevent future problems helps everyone—the elder, the caregivers, and all members of the family.

Every family can improve its systems. Make the effort now to put supports in place so that elders and their caregivers get the help and resources they need. There is a tremendous amount of information available on this topic on the Internet. The websites Helpguide.org (search for "Elder Abuse and Neglect") and NCEA.aoa.gov (by the National Center on Elder Abuse) were particularly helpful sources of information for this chapter, as was the organization HESSCO Elder Services (www.hessco.org/protective_services).

9

INCLUDING THE ELDER'S VOICE

When facing family decisions, sometimes family members struggle with how best to learn about and honor the wishes of an elder without causing undue stress on their loved one. In this chapter we'll discuss ways you and your family can help ensure that your elder's voice is included in any decision-making process that will impact the elder and his or her happiness, comfort, finances, health, or legacy.

REMEMBER YOUR CHANGING PERSPECTIVE

As aging issues begin to impact our parents, many of us may perceive Mom or Dad as having diminished capacity from some former state of competence, control, and charisma. But let's remember, back "then" they appeared to be on top of this mountain in part because we were younger, less powerful, and less discerning—literally looking up to them. So, while our analytic abilities about them were exaggerated upward in our youth, let's guard against overreacting negatively now.

Even if your perspective is clear eyed, remember that not all older individuals have capacity issues. People don't need protection from conflict merely because they have reached a certain age. Explore your age biases before you begin a decision-making process. You can help to make your parents' aging process the dignified experience it is capable of being.

ELDER PARTICIPATION PRINCIPLES

When you and your family are faced with decision-making challenges around elder issues, consider the eight **Elder Participation Principles** on the following pages. The central idea here is to explore what you can do to both honor your elder's right to make his or her own decisions and include your elder's voice in important decision-making processes. You want to allow Mom or Dad to be fully heard to the best of their ability without doing harm.

PRINCIPLE 1: Consider creating room for participation even if there is diminished capacity from a medical or legal perspective.

You may be embarking on a family conversation in which a senior is fully capable of making their own decisions and participating in a decision-making process. If, however, the individual has been placed under guardianship or conservatorship—or if you are concerned about an elder's capabilities because you've noticed a change in their ability to stay with a conversation, voice their opinions, or fully participate in discussions—you will want to consider what their role in the discussion might be. This change in abilities certainly does not mean that they shouldn't be involved at all. There's a wide continuum of people's ability to participate meaningfully in a discussion or a decision-making process, and we strongly encourage you to look for ways to include your elder's voice in the process as much as possible. This may range from full participation (with or without a support person or advocate also present) to having an advocate or surrogate speak for them if they are no longer able to participate directly. If there is less than full ability to participate, you may also be able to bring their voice into the room by seeking opinions and checking in with them at various points in the process.

A guiding principle in our practice is to seek to maximize everyone's capacity to participate while doing no harm.

We have worked with some families who have honored a parent by having him or her physically present in a family meeting even when the parent seemed to have little or no capacity to actively participate or understand what was going on. While these specific situations have been rare, what was important to the family was the respectful tone in the room with the parent present. In some cases, family members feel that conversations become more civil and thoughtful when the parent, while possibly unable to understand the words spoken, can feel and respond to nonverbal interactions and emotions expressed. Clearly, if you are considering such a scenario, you want to be sensitive to the elder's condition and be careful not to put him or her in a position where they become overly confused or upset by the conversation and/or topics raised.

If an elder is able to participate in only a limited way, be sure that their "voice" is also included through other means.

PRINCIPLE 2: While legal competence is decided by a court, in real life you may find yourself in a position where you need to assess someone's capacity to appropriately participate in a decision-making process.

Here are some tips:

- Begin by getting a sense of a person's understanding of a problem. Her memory? His reasoning? Are they able to follow a conversation and respond to relevant questions?
- Don't judge or make assumptions about anyone before talking with that person about the issue under consideration.
- Remember that the "right to make bad decisions" has been upheld in many states. It is not necessarily a sign of incompetence.
- We all should assume capacity first.

PRINCIPLE 3: Consider the kind of process you and your family are in.

Is it a negotiation or simply a conversation? The capacity to make an agreement is different from the capacity to have a conversation. You and your siblings can learn a lot from your parents by engaging in soft, nonthreatening discussions on important issues.

PRINCIPLE 4: To maximize the capacity to participate, ask ALL family members if any accommodations would be helpful.

Here is a checklist that we mediators use. While all points may not apply to you, keep them in mind as you plan any family discussion. Chapter 10, Family Meetings, will go into this list in more detail:

- Select a familiar, comfortable location.
- Ask about best time of day.
- Be sensitive to length of sessions/breaks.
- Consider lighting and using larger print for shared documents.
- Eliminate glare through seating, use of blinds.
- Choose language with care. Avoid legalese and jargon.
- Speak slowly/clearly with lower pitch of voice.
- Pace the conversation, use a calm tone, with simple and short questions. But don't be patronizing.
- Remove background noise and visual distractions.
- Build trust with social conversation.
- Have snacks and beverages available at the table and plan for the family to share a meal together if at all possible.
- Think about using written summaries, flip charts, lists, diagrams, maps, and visual aids.
- Allow time for understanding. Use patient repetition as needed.
- Respond to the emotions of the participants if their words are unclear.
- Ask the speaker's permission before asking others to help you understand him or her.
- Don't talk about a participant in the third person.
- Don't ask questions which require memory when memory loss is an issue.
- Be aware of tone, respectfulness, and body language.
- Encourage advocates to attend: friends, clergy, geriatric care managers (GCMs), lawyers, etc.

Even as you begin to focus in on how best to include the elder(s) in your family in a decision-making process, it is important to keep your analytic lens wide open for a while. It is a rare family that doesn't have other participants with issues that can impact a decision-making process. Dad may be forgetful and need to take a break now and then, but son Freddy drinks way too much and has a hard time focusing. Mom may have some hearing loss and need you all to pay attention to volume, pitch, and direction of your speech, but daughter Suzie may have some vision loss and need documents printed in large print to be able to best read them.

PRINCIPLE 5: Partial Presence.

Be open to the possibility that, in some situations, it may be in your parents' best interests for family members to have a series of conversations, some of which your parents participate in, and some of which they "sit out on."

In our mediation practice, we would rather err in the direction of including the elder in all conversations because we believe, wherever possible, it's important to have each voice in the room. But sometimes participation by everyone all the time doesn't make sense. For instance, should Mom be at every family meeting now that her tolerance for conflict is very low? Or should Dad have to sit through a conversation about how hard it is to provide for all his needs?

Some families decide to meet without parents to get preliminary bickering out of the way and to consider a process for making decisions. Then the elder is involved at points when key decisions are being discussed and made. If it is not possible for the elder to be present at the meeting, an advocate—such as a social worker, geriatric care manager, or personal attorney—could possibly speak for the elder after taking the time to get to know him and his wants and needs.

PRINCIPLE 6: Be open and transparent.

You don't have to be secretive about meeting without your parents. If Mom and Dad understand that they will be fully informed, they may surprise you by how comfortable they are with entrusting some of the decision-making about some specific issues to their adult children. Remember, good old shuttle diplomacy may help here, too. A trusted sibling can go to your parents and seek input, relay proposed decisions and questions, or just report on the process.

PRINCIPLE 7: Recognize your own biases about your aging parent(s).

Acknowledge the fact that "I'm making assumptions." We rarely have perfect information and total clarity and therefore continually make assumptions in our day-to-day decision-making. So assumption making is an important process; yet if done without mindfulness, our biases can creep in to influence our thinking and make our assumptions inaccurate. The key is to be aware of our biases and the assumptions we are making, and to be open to new information that may change our way of thinking. Remember your *GPS* from Chapter 1.

- Check assumptions out—are they true? If you think Dad is lonely, maybe it's because he fits your profile of what lonely should look like, not his. For example, after an active life Dad may revel in long stretches of solitude and quiet. Or maybe he is lonely. You will only know if you can learn how he honestly feels.
- Be curious! Too often we don't engage in simple conversations about the normal rhythms of life that may have fascinating undercurrents. Dad may take the exact same walk each morning at the exact same time because he loves to flirt with the crossing guard at the end of the block, not because he is becoming obsessive.
- What biases (both positive and negative) do we hold? Make a list. Be brutally honest. You don't have to share the list with anybody, and your self-reflection can help you be much more effective in dealing with your family.

Our biases can influence not only our thought processes but our behaviors as well. Work to AVOID these behaviors that can show age bias, and challenge the assumptions that underlie them. Here are some examples that may seem all too familiar:

- Not paying attention to, or not valuing, what the elder is saying
- Interrupting, finishing sentences, or speaking for the older person
- Speaking about an older person in the room in the third person
- Using overly simple language ("baby talk")

PRINCIPLE 8: Honor your parents' culture around decision-making.

Your parents come from a different generation with different norms than yours. In making estate-planning decisions, for instance, what happens when Dad is even more private about his affairs with his family than he is with his friends? Maybe you should think about when to back off and allow Dad to figure things out his way. You might simply acknowledge to your Dad that you respect his right to privacy and to do what he wants, and that you also want him to know that you are open to discussing things if he wishes—then leave it at that; you've opened the door without pressuring him for further conversation.

Or, what happens if both your parents refuse to consider planning any housing option other than "staying in this house until they carry us out feet first"? Rather than jumping to consider how you could break through such barriers, maybe you should explore if you even have the right to interfere.

Look for ways to honor and support your parents' decisions. For example, families faced with the situation above are finding that there are many imaginative ways to comfortably maintain elders in their own homes. You might consider hiring a geriatric care manager to do an assessment about their needs and options for "aging in place," as a way to help them be successful in the environment of their choice.

DETERMINING PRIOR WISHES

If you and your family are in conflict following the death of a parent (or after they have become unable to express their wishes), consider this person's prior wishes. Were Mom and Dad clear about bequests—including both financial assets and personal items? According to bankrate.com, only about 43% of Americans have a will and/or leave clear instructions that make it easy for their families to avoid struggling with some key uncommunicated issue such as burial instructions or who gets what.

So the sleuth work often has to begin once the body has been slipped into the ground or the ashes spread. But what if even these wishes aren't clear? What to do? Empower everyone to take part in the process with the goal of determining what were the wishes, values, and goals expressed by this person in the past. Remember, best guesses everyone can agree on are better than giving up when no absolute truth can be found.

When all your sources provide little or no help, ask your family <u>how</u> they want to determine what Mom or Dad would have wanted—discuss which "objective standards" (recollections, documents, etc.) they want to use to measure this. Mom loved gardening so maybe you will spread her ashes at her favorite garden spot. Dad loved tinkering in his garage and making lovely furniture. Maybe you can all agree to make a donation of cash and tools to the local technical high school.

Perhaps your parents weren't the best role models in terms of generosity and treating all family members fairly. If it's possible for the next generation to agree, you all can, of course, consider doing what you think is fair even when you know your deceased parents might have handled things differently. For example, even if your father treated adopted grandchildren differently in life, you and your siblings might agree to fully recognize adopted children or blended families when distributing assets from the estate.

And when all else fails, remember that there are great resources available to help you. Check out the Resource section at the end of this guide for additional ideas.

—•—

Don't let your fear of capacity issues override your desire to hear an elder's voice. Remember that not all elders have capacity issues and, even if they do, there may be ways for them to participate. Follow the listed principles to guide you and your family towards maximizing your elder's participation.

10

FAMILY MEETINGS

Family meetings can work. When well designed, they provide an efficient forum for families to sit down together to discuss and resolve the tough issues they are confronting. If managed properly, a well-run family meeting can ease future decision-making and strengthen ongoing family relationships. The goals of the meeting—whether formal or informal—will vary by family, but in addition to resolving current issues, family meetings can lay the groundwork for better communication and improved collaboration in the future.

TIMING AND LOCATION

So, when should family meetings be held? For the most part, the timing depends on the complicated schedules of all the family members. If there are several siblings in your family, you may all have to be patient as you work out the timing and location for a meeting. And don't be surprised if changes in work schedules or other obligations occasionally require rescheduling and a do-over that can cause frustration.

For many families, holidays are ideal—siblings may already be coming from afar to visit, and most everyone may have time off from work. While this can be convenient, remember that in-laws are often in the mix during the holidays and some siblings may have other plans. And the costs associated with holiday travel can be problematic. Furthermore, for some, holiday time is supposed to be kept light and social, and the idea of discussing serious topics doesn't fit.

Your family might like to schedule an annual meeting over the same weekend every year. While some family members might consider this to be too inflexible, regularly scheduled meetings—whenever they are held—can become a tradition which strengthens family bonds over time.

The location of your meeting should be carefully thought out. Choose a location where everyone will be comfortable and able to talk freely. Meeting at the law offices of your brother's attorney may not sit well if there are trust issues among your family members. And meeting in your sister's dining room could make you uncomfortable if you were hoping to address your sister's unwillingness to provide funds for Dad's new home health aide. A neutral setting can provide a level playing field for all participants. Consider the conference room at the assisted living facility where Mom lives, or a private meeting room at a hotel or restaurant. Meeting at the home of your parent(s) can also work as long as there are no issues of neutrality posed by that location.

You may want to gather at a vacation spot like a beach area or near your family's favorite mountain resort. This can work well and can add the atmosphere of a "family retreat" to the events—even giving opportunities to combine work and play—but it might also be hard to get everyone inside for an extended meeting, so keep this in mind when selecting a "fun" location.

With siblings living far apart and having busy schedules, finding a convenient time and place for everyone can be a challenge, especially if an elder cannot travel. The logistics of setting up a meeting can be as complicated, if not more complicated, than having the actual meeting. To help, there are several online scheduling tools (e.g., MeetingWizard.com and Doodle.com) that can make the process of finding a time to meet quite painless. The bottom line here is that there is no right or wrong answer—whatever time and place works best for you all is what matters.

WHO SHOULD PARTICIPATE?

Participation in a family meeting should be voluntary. There are no hard and fast rules here, but we feel strongly that all stakeholders (those impacted by the decisions of the group) should be invited to have a voice at the table. This means that even if someone does not physically attend all meetings, his voice should be heard in some form. He may participate by phone. She may have a surrogate represent her, or she may wish to simply come in, "say hello," and make a brief statement before leaving others to do the heavy lifting.

Sometimes spouses wish to attend these meetings. While for some families this may just seem natural, for other families—as you might imagine—this can cause friction. Perhaps not all siblings have a spouse, but some may have a long-term life partner or may be in a newly serious relationship. Some spouses may have a particular involvement with the family or a care-giving responsibility that others do not. It's also not unusual for one spouse to be disliked or not trusted by some siblings. And even when there are good relationships with all the spouses and partners, sometimes family members prefer to restrict these very personal discussions to the members of their family of origin.

The same dynamics can apply to the grandchildren. They may have a stake in the outcome—for example, whether the family vacation home gets sold—but should they have a say? What if some grandchildren are in their 20's or 30's and others are still young children? Every family situation is different, and again your family will need to decide what makes sense for you all in order for everyone to be comfortable with the assembled group.

In family meetings, adult siblings often see themselves as representing a larger constituency—like their spouses and their children. It's important for everyone to be transparent about this since the siblings may need to "get approval" on some level from their constituents in order for any decisions to be completely upheld without unpleasant consequences. The happiness of the extended family members can be a common interest of the siblings and elders at the table. It can be useful to work out a way together to best communicate any decisions to those who did not have an opportunity to par-ticipate, and to share the interests and options which were jointly discussed.

As we discussed in Chapter 9, although an elder's situation is often at the heart of the conversation, it sometimes makes sense for him or her to attend only part of the meeting. Knowing your own family's dynamic, you might be concerned that having Mom hear her children arguing with each other could be damaging to her and her relationships with her kids. And nobody wants to hear that they are a burden or that the cost of their care is putting a financial strain on the family. That said, when the decisions do directly involve the elder, we suggest you do your best to accommodate the needs of the elder to enable him or her to participate at least for part of the meeting. Consider the accommodations mentioned in the previous chapter to increase the possibility that the elder can participate. And remember the principle of seeking to maximize participation while doing no harm.

Sometimes, regardless of when and where the meeting is held, someone still cannot attend. As mentioned in Chapter 3, current technology offers many options that can help in this situation. In the context of family meetings, technology can allow a sibling who otherwise couldn't participate in a discussion to be included. For example, Skype® or a simple speakerphone can give someone far away the opportunity to be part of all discussions and maybe even "see" his or her family members.

DISCUSSION TOPICS

There is a wide range of topics that may be discussed at family meetings. For some families, a parent's health and safety is the primary topic that needs attention. For others, the discussion may be centered on financial concerns. It can be very helpful to have an agenda developed ahead of time with input from all participants.

And if there are difficult topics—those "elephants in the room"— consider when and whether to name these as well. It can often be helpful to get these topics out in the open, but timing can be important. You may first want to begin building skills, success, and trust with some simpler topics and decision-making. A good strategy can be to start with the "low hanging fruit" to build momentum, but remember that issues that fester are likely to only get worse, so don't push the tough topics off the table indefinitely.

In our work with families we find some recurring themes that surface in family meetings, including:

- Dad's/Mom's happiness
- Maintaining his/her autonomy
- Safety and health concerns
- Residence decisions—where will an elder live?
- Financial and estate planning

- Caregiving roles and responsibilities
- Sharing vacation homes and other property among family members
- Family dynamics and ongoing communication
- Decision-making processes now and in the future
- Questions of fairness

Any or all of the above topics—and more—can be at play at the same time, potentially creating a tight knot of indecision. Given the multitude and complexity of topics, and the challenges of family communication, it is no wonder that family decision-making can be so difficult, and that family meetings can be so important.

WHAT ABOUT CONFIDENTIALITY?

This brings us to the matter of privacy and confidentiality. You will all want to be very clear about what information can be shared outside the meeting and with whom. You may all decide that you are free to reveal anything to your spouses and life partners, your lawyers, your financial advisors, etc. But you may not want friends, children, or other associates to know anything about your discussions except that you had a family meeting and it went well. You and your family should address this matter early on and revisit it at the end of your meeting.

INVOLVING OUTSIDE ADVISORS

Families often rely upon outside professionals to provide advice and advocacy as needed in order to negotiate informed and reasoned solutions. The advice of attorneys, financial advisors, geriatric care managers, and others can be indispensable. That said, give careful thought to how best to bring in the advice of a professional. Rarely are these individuals perceived to be neutral by everyone, especially those family members who feel their voices are not being heard. Depending in part on your family's relationship with the advisor, consider how much of the meeting (if any) the advisor might attend, what his/her role will be (e.g., to make a presentation only, and/ or to participate in discussion of options, etc.), and what other ways their advice might be sought. And if the advisor is advocating for some siblings, consider ways that other siblings may be supported as well. For example, if an attorney participates in the process—particularly if representing anyone other than the elder—it's not uncommon for two or more attorneys to participate, each representing different sibling(s) in the family.

RUNNING THE MEETING

When you embark on a family meeting, be clear about your objectives: for all participants to identify their own interests, understand the interests of others, and consider all the options available. Your goal is to create workable, enduring, and equitable solutions for whatever problems your family may face.

It is important to set a time frame and to prioritize topics so the meeting doesn't go on interminably. Be mindful of everyone's needs. While we may be most sensitive to the needs of the elder, others may need some consideration too. Your sister may need to leave in time for an evening shift, your brother may need some time to check in with his team at the office, or you may need a break for some fresh air and an afternoon cup of coffee.

Although this may seem trite, having good snacks available can help participants keep focused and can also lift the mood in the room. It cannot be overstated that sharing meals can do wonders to rebuild a sense of family and restore good will. If time permits, consider building a meal into your time together.

Most importantly, use the Active Listening skills discussed in Chapter 3. While it's even more challenging to use these skills in a group than in one-to-one conversation, it can also be remarkably effective. Take the time to reflect back to others what you are hearing and seek clarity. When it is time to give your own opinion, be transparent that that's what you are doing and state it in terms of your interests so that others can more easily hear it.

CONSIDER HAVING A NEUTRAL FACILITATOR
AT THE TABLE

Just as you consider involving outside advisors, consider having a neutral person at the table as well. A neutral facilitator is often needed to gain the trust of all participants, to help ensure that all perspectives are considered, and to keep the meeting on track.

More often than not, the issues to be addressed in family meetings are intertwined, and this complexity can be overwhelming. Individual family members who are not trained in facilitating meetings—particularly meetings on complex, emotional topics—can get bogged down in the complexity and become ineffective discussion leaders. This is compounded by the fact that they have a real stake in the outcome of the meeting. This does not mean that you and your family can't manage what we call a "graceful transition" on your own, but don't look at the need to involve professionals as failure. Family decision-making is a challenging process, and there are professionals trained to help you.

Mediators trained in helping family members with complex decision-making processes can work with you to establish an agenda, keep the conversation focused, and ensure that each voice in the room is heard. If, after exploring options, you all agree on some next steps and decisions, the mediator can help you document these so that you have a record of your progress to refer to in the future.

We encourage families to hold regular meetings to hear and understand what everyone thinks and wants *before* damaging conflicts erupt. Family meetings provide the forum for all to be heard, share their views, and learn from each other. Respectful, ongoing communication strengthens family bonds, builds relationships, and provides the basis for smooth and effective decision-making at times of transition.

11

....

COMMUNICATION CHALLENGES

Communication is the mothers' milk of decision-making and conflict resolution. It's the cause of many disputes and the source of all resolutions. Knowing where we got into trouble and how to find our way out means looking at how we have communicated with one another and how we can do better.

SAYING AND SHOWING WHAT YOU MEAN

Why is it often so difficult to make decisions as a family? We know that you may have different interests and that some family members could be working with faulty assumptions, or they might be restricted by myths or memories or distrust. We've talked about all of these challenges and more. But the hurdle that consistently presents the greatest difficulty for adult family members, siblings and aging parents alike, is communication.

When we are in conflict, we usually think that we have already <u>repeatedly</u> communicated our perceptions, our values, and our concerns to others. And we know that we have, on several occasions, clearly explained our well-thought-out solutions. We may be offended that nobody seemed to take us seriously, or respected our judgment, or even gave us the courtesy of a response. This can happen for many reasons. Sometimes it's intentional, and sometimes it's not. And so much goes on "between the lines"; unspoken communication can be missed or misunderstood, thus derailing a conversation.

When we are facing tough decisions or find ourselves in difficult situations, our tensions rise and we become less able to communicate. We sometimes say things that we don't really mean, but that we think will bolster our case or shield us from criticism. You might say that you have no interest in continuing a relationship with your two sisters when, in fact, you want nothing more than for them to simply apologize to you so that the family can get back to normal. You can imagine how "reading between the lines" becomes even more difficult as more people are involved.

In a heated dispute, each family member may present his or her case (*"We just can't share ownership of that house without bickering all the time"*) and demand that others accept that they are "right." (*"You all know it's true! Look what happened last summer when Roy brought his fraternity brothers and left the place trashed. It took Joan and me all weekend to clean it up, and we missed two great beach days with our kids!"*) Arguments generally ensue regarding who's right or wrong based on the "facts."

The problem is that conversations then become about the perceived facts, not about what's really important to each person. Workable solutions can become elusive when individual perspectives and interests are couched behind "facts." While you believe that Roy acted irresponsibly by leaving such a mess, it's possible that there was some other explanation. Maybe Roy was not aware that you were coming the next weekend, and he had planned to clean the place when he returned in two weeks. Rather than arguing about the past, you would be better served by focusing on interests: yours—that the house be clean when you arrive, and Roy's—that he be made aware of everyone's schedule so he could plan appropriately. With this understanding moving forward, Roy would know that if he could not return before the next occupants were due to arrive he should either hire a cleaner or clean the place himself before racing off for the last ferry. Focusing on interests and "unpacking assumptions" will set you on a course toward resolution far more effectively than arguing about the past.

So much of what makes things difficult in families comes from poor or misunderstood communication. In its most basic form communication involves the sender of a message and a recipient of that message. The message begins as an idea the sender wants to convey, but—when received—may be "read" as something different from what was intended. The words you choose to use when sending a message, your tone of voice, and your body language will all affect how your message is received. So you need to be especially careful when you are not communicating in person, as you don't have the benefit of facial expressions and body language to help convey what you really want to say. If you're writing an email, the punctuation and specific words may carry greater meaning. Have you ever sent an angry email written in all CAPS? If so, then you may already well know that this form of communication can feel cathartic at the time, but rarely leads to a positive outcome.

So while it seems like it should be the simplest thing in the world to say what you mean and have others hear and understand you, it may be much more complicated than that, and the consequences of miscommunications can be far reaching. So many things can go wrong. If you, as the sender, are frustrated or angry, your message will be impacted. If you make a statement but your tone and body language are not perceived as being "in sync" with your words, your message may be received as something entirely different from what you intended. So think about the message you want to get across, how you want to deliver it (in person, over the phone, via email), and how best to structure that message so it will be received as you intend.

Consider carefully what you want to impart to your family. What do you want to tell them, and what do you <u>not</u> want to tell them? Similarly, what do you want to hear from them? What do you want to ask? When conversations are important, it's always a good idea to explicitly check in with others to be certain that you are reading them accurately. Let others know that you want to avoid miscommunication. Slow down the pace, and summarize what you think you've heard. Ask for clarification and check for accuracy regularly.

It's also important to be clear with yourself about which topics are likely to be easy and which ones will be difficult to bring up. Think about the words you use—are there some hot-button words that you know will trigger a reaction? Maybe your mom is very sensitive about your brother's past employment troubles, and she shuts down whenever anyone implies she has given him more than his fair share of financial help. It's not that you shouldn't bring up a sensitive topic; you just need to be mindful of what reaction it may cause so you can be well prepared to provide the necessary "cushioning"—like, *"I know that this topic is uncomfortable for you and that you would rather we not discuss it. At the same time, it's important to me, and I'd like for all of us to figure this out together."*

YOUR COMMUNICATION SYSTEM

Communication may have been an issue for you and your family in the past. So you may all decide that it would be helpful to create a communication plan going forward. This could be a scheduled monthly meeting in person or by phone. It might be an agreement to have an email exchange every Sunday, or simply a promise to respond to non-emergency phone messages and emails within an agreed upon time period. For some families, an annual face-to-face meeting with a neutral facilitator is incorporated into an overall communication plan. Your family may want to try out various communication systems before settling on the one that works best.

Implementing a plan for ongoing communication—whether an informal agreement to be responsive to each other's emails and calls within a certain timeframe, or a more formal regular meeting schedule—is essential and should be part of every family's dispute resolution process.

Communication is a two-edged sword, especially when a family is already in distress. Remember that old game of "telephone" where the message changes and becomes unrecognizable as it travels from person to person within a group? While we need to share information in order to create consensus and plan for the future, we want to be careful to avoid misunderstandings that cause damage. Effective communication requires commitment, time, and attention.

12

MAKING DECISIONS

Family systems are like organizations. They have leaders, followers, coalitions, and—of course—internal politics. Like any organization, they can benefit from a decision-making and dispute resolution system that incorporates some of the thinking currently employed in thoughtfully structured businesses, universities, and government organizations.

By looking to the field of Dispute Systems Design (DSD), you and your family can create your own smoothly operating structure for making important decisions and resolving disagreements in the future. Together you can develop a roadmap for managing your process of decision-making, using a common language that reduces misunderstandings and promotes communication.

So what is your family's current dispute resolution system? Do the wishes of your oldest brother always trump others when disputes arise? Or maybe Mom still rules with an iron hand. In some families, the caregiver daughter makes all the day-to-day eldercare decisions while her out-of-state brother controls the purse strings. In many families, disputes are avoided whenever possible, and decisions are made on an *ad hoc* basis. Sometimes these models work (if no one complains about the outcome), and sometimes ill feelings and growing distrust are the result.

It's a good idea to review your dispute system in order to assess how well it really works for your family. Before you can begin to hope for improvement, you all will need to consider how it has worked in the past and how you would each like it to work in the future. And as you think about how you'd like to make it better, consider incorporating elements of the consensus building model described below.

Let's revisit one of the families introduced in an earlier chapter, in which you and your sister Amanda were exploring what to do about Mom's driving. You were worried about Mom's safety and the safety of others on the roadways, but Amanda was initially reluctant to pursue this, as she did not wish to jeopardize Mom's ability to maintain her active social life and sense of independence. In truth, you shared this concern and you also didn't want Mom to be angry or upset with you. So, now you've decided that it's time to have THE conversation.

PREPARING FOR CONVERSATIONS

The odds of success in an important conversation improve considerably with preparation. You can think of a difficult conversation as a negotiation; you wouldn't go into a business negotiation without preparing for it, and you shouldn't go into a family conversation unprepared either.

Consider what your interests are, and consider others' interests as well.

What is important to you and what do you hope to achieve? Remember not to confuse your interests with your positions. Once you're clear on what you want, think about what the others want. Can you find any common ground? What potential options exist to meet your interests as well as theirs? Being clear about these interests ahead of time will help prepare you for your conversations.

Think about your current family relationships and the types of relationships you would like to have in the future.

In any family conflict, your family relationships, your level of trust, and your ability to communicate with your family members each plays a large role in how your decision-making process unfolds.

What are your relationships like now? Can this conversation result in an improved relationship with your mother or your sister? Do you want it to? What type of relationship do your children have with their cousins, and how will they be affected by your decisions or lack thereof? How you answer these questions will affect how you approach the conversation.

In your conversation with your sister and with your mom, because you genuinely care for each other and have a high level of trust—and you all want your good relationships to continue—you are likely to be able to work together productively to uncover shared interests and develop options to satisfy those interests. If there were no trust and a general dislike or disrespect for one another, decision-making would become more difficult.

Consider your alternatives.

Once you have thought through your interests and your desired relationships, you will want to prepare the best possible case for the delicate negotiations that lie ahead. While you must be genuinely prepared to negotiate a mutually agreed upon resolution, it is important to fully consider what else you could do or what might happen if no decisions or agreements are made. What can you do if your family members will not cooperate with you? The stronger your alternatives, the more power you have in the conversation.

Remember your BATNA, your Best Alternative to a Negotiated Agreement—we discussed this in Chapter 6. If you know that there's something you can do on your own, you are less likely to agree to a resolution that does not fully meet your interests. Similarly, think about what your family members' alternatives might be. What can they do on their own—without needing your buy-in or consent—if you don't agree with what they want? If you know they have alternatives they can pursue that you don't want to see happen, that will motivate you to work harder for resolution.

So before entering into your discussions with Amanda and Mom, it will be important for you to consider what the alternatives might be if your family doesn't reach an agreement.

Mom could continue driving without limitation, but she might get lost again or she might have an accident in which someone was seriously hurt. You could just go ahead and set up an account with a local taxi company and then demand that Mom turn over her keys—but that could be very upsetting for her, especially if she did not believe that a taxi service would provide her with a good way to maintain her social life and community involvement. And this way of going about things would probably feel disrespectful to both of you. Besides, what if the taxi company proved unreliable? You would feel responsible, and your mother would be left in a tough situation. As far as your sister goes, you realize that Amanda could continue to ignore your concerns—except that she would never want to risk having Mom's safety compromised. *No great alternatives for anyone on this list.*

It looks like you all have a lot to lose if your discussions are not successful. That's good. You each have reason to work together toward a resolution.

Respectfully invite others to the conversation.

Be thoughtful about how to bring others into the conversation in a way that doesn't make demands or put people on the defensive. Often, articulating your own interest in having a conversation, and acknowledging what you know so far of the interests of others, can help.

So to encourage Mom to have "the conversation," you and Amanda might start with something like: *"Mom, we know how important it is for you to continue living a busy, full life. And we want you to come and go to your activities with as much ease as possible. We're also both concerned about your safety on the road. Could we all get together to talk about how to make decisions as a family regarding your continued independence and your safety?"* Expressing your interest in Mom's happiness, your concern for her welfare, and your willingness to be collaborative are all important in creating an "invitation" to talk that is likely to bear fruit.

CONSENSUS BUILDING

So what decision-making process will work for your family?

In our practice we aren't fans of voting. In fact, we think voting a simple "Yay/Nay" generally does more harm than good in family situations. This is because when there's a vote, there are winners and losers. In your family you might have seen the same configuration of winners and losers for almost every past vote. What this does, over time, is set up a hierarchy and power coalition that can lead to an even more fractured family. And it's not uncommon for the people on the side that loses to do whatever they can to undermine the decision that was voted on, making the "resolution" unstable and unsustainable.

Let's say you and your brother and sister, Jeff and Marissa, are trying to figure out how best to allocate your father's care needs among the three of you, now that he has broken his hip.

How are you going to make decisions here? How will you agree on what services or support Dad needs? Who should pay for what? And should your sister be paid or get other compensation to give care when she has been living rent free in Dad's house? What if she needs the money and others don't?

If you and Jeff and Marissa voted and decided that each person would chip in equally for the cost of Dad's caregiver, and the decision did not feel equitable to Marissa, she could simply withhold her payments in the future. Then you'd be back to square one with less family trust and optimism this time around. Simply out-voting some family members does not address interests, and does not create workable options for the future.

We believe that the **Consensus Building** approach is one of the best systems of decision-making for families. It was developed by Lawrence Susskind of the Consensus Building Institute in Cambridge, Massachusetts, for use in the public arena. Consensus Building puts the responsibility on each participant of a decision-making process to contribute to building a solution.

The way it can work with families is as follows: The group starts by identifying individual interests and then looks for common interests. Everyone brainstorms options. Once an array of options is on the table, these options are discussed and evaluated, with participants looking for the possible merits of each suggestion. Generally, one or two options emerge as potential solutions. At this point, everyone ranks the options on a six-point scale where A represents, *"I wholeheartedly agree"* and F represents, *"I cannot be part of this decision and must block it."* The other letters between A and F represent more moderate views, like, *"It's a good idea, and I'm very supportive"*; *"I can support this"*; *"I have reservations and want to talk more about it"*; and *"I have serious concerns, and we must talk more about it."*

The goal is for each participant to feel that the final solution is something that they can live with, even if it does not provide everything they want. In the event that there are one or two parties who have serious reservations or who cannot agree to a proposed solution, it becomes their responsibility to explain to the group why this particular solution, or more specifically, what parts of it, do not meet their interests. Furthermore, they will be responsible for suggesting changes that would meet their own interests without losing the support of others. In this process, individuals cannot simply derail a potentially workable solution, nor can they walk away feeling unheard or left out of the decision. It is a process that keeps the discussion moving forward.

So regarding caregiving for your father, rather than dividing the costs between you as above, you might propose to your siblings that your family hire a caregiver and that the costs could be covered by selling the undeveloped land in Nova Scotia that you all inherited from your grandfather. Let's say, however, that Jeff thinks the land will appreciate in the future and he can't imagine selling it now. Your sister Marissa doesn't think your father needs expensive care at all. But she points out that it might possibly be useful to have those funds available one day if it becomes necessary to finance other things like structural accommodations to Dad's house. Looking at the option of selling the land to pay for care, you might wholeheartedly agree with it, Jeff would block it, and Marissa would have serious concerns.

Going through a Consensus Building process, you'd ask your siblings what changes to your proposal would be needed to make it acceptable to them. Your brother might agree that more care is needed and that it has to be financed, but he would insist that it be done another way. Your sister might further define what she thinks Dad's needs are. You could then brainstorm how else to finance those needs. As options are fleshed out, you would continue to use the Consensus Building scale to evaluate which options have support and which don't, and keep revising until you come up with a solution that everyone is comfortable with.

SAVING FACE

This brings us to the matter of "saving face." We all know that saving face is important. Humiliation, simple embarrassment, or even the anticipation of either can cause people to react in an offensive or defensive manner. Obviously, this pattern is to be avoided when our goal is to resolve a dispute or to collaborate with others on critical decisions. So ask yourself what purpose it serves to remind your sister that she has always been hypersensitive about money issues. She might be so humiliated as to get up and walk out, or she might simply "punish" you by being unwilling to listen to your interests when you need her to do so.

In family discussions, protecting everyone's honor and dignity (and the honor of the family itself) by always showing respect can be vital to a successful process. And when concessions are made, they should be framed in a manner that highlights fairness so that no parties feel that they have been taken advantage of or demeaned by the process. After all, if someone feels that he has lost face, the ongoing result can be that he may, over time, show his resentment by working to undermine the resolutions that were achieved in the family discussions. Not only does "saving face" contribute to a successful negotiation, but also to a more durable resolution.

COMMITMENTS

Commitments that you make to each other—whether through the Consensus Building process or through any other process—need to be realistic. Nobody should agree to do something beyond what they can realistically deliver. For example, can you continue to spend every Saturday running errands and doing chores for Dad? Will your sister Marissa truly be able to be there or call him four times a day to remind him to take his medications? If you each can do these things, then go ahead. If not, the "agreement" to provide all the caregiving yourselves won't last, and it still needs more work!

Be sure to discuss the feasibility of any commitments you make and try to include some "what ifs" in your plan. What if any one of these commitments isn't met? What would that look like? What would you all do next?

DEFINING SUCCESS ALONG THE WAY

Defining the success of your family meeting(s) depends on what you were trying to achieve. Some families want a final decision made on a particular topic. Others want to have a civilized conversation that begins to approach a solution. Some are looking for a signed contract, while others want a list of possible options or the beginnings of a plan to move forward. Still others are looking for a communication system or clear decision-making process put in place so that there will be a structure to make decisions on an as-needed basis in the future.

We have no one definition for success, just as we have no one definition for a happy family. It is always helpful to be clear from the start what your goals are, and it is also important to look at what you have achieved in any conversation—even if it is simply that you all were able to say what was on your minds and that you each felt that the others listened and understood you. Just feeling heard is a big step on the road to collaborative decision-making.

If you can frame "success" as a journey, not an end point, you and your family are more likely to stay engaged. Productive conversations are your interim destinations (your "via points" on your *GPS*) along the road to resolution.

—•—

Sometimes *how* you make decisions as a family is just as important as *what* decisions you make. When everyone feels that they can support a resolution and uphold their commitments, the resulting plan is more likely to be durable. And remember, you may well be confronted with more matters that require joint consideration in the future, whether due to an elder's continued decline, changes in financial circumstances, end-of-life issues, or even burial and funeral decisions. Consider your decision-making process carefully as it will likely have long-term implications.

13

WHAT OTHER FAMILIES DO

In our mediation practice, we generally avoid offering ideas or suggesting solutions that other families have designed in their deliberations. This is because resolutions tend to be more powerful, effective, and durable if they are developed by family members themselves, uniquely tailored for their own family's situation. A family's self-generated ideas will be the "right" options for that particular complex family situation, and these solutions will have the best chance of lasting if the parties fully own the decision-making process.

If you are not working with a mediator or a conflict resolution professional at this time, you will need to organize a family decision-making process yourselves. And we understand that you might like to have at your disposal a range of ideas to inspire you and to help you and your family be more effective and efficient in your decision-making. So in this chapter we will share some of the options that other families have developed to resolve their particular conflicts—in the hope that these ideas may stimulate your own creative brainstorming of new options that you and your family craft together.

USING THIRD-PARTY VALUATIONS

Is your family struggling with property distribution issues? Is the monetary value of the property at issue? Even when emotional attachment to certain property seems to be most important, you might still want to have objects and property appraised before you begin any decision-making process.

Real estate is the most obvious category, but potentially valuable household items that are being distributed can be appraised as well. It's amazing how things we think are valuable simply are not. That Hummel collection may be worth a third of what your mother paid for it. Any furniture that isn't an antique is worth very little; and don't expect the value of that 72 piece set of silverware to have appreciated in recent years. And then there are the things you think are worthless that aren't: some old toys and Mom's Hungarian dinnerware. We've all seen Antiques Roadshow® and the surprises that are highlighted weekly. So appraise, appraise, appraise, but remember that an appraisal does not guarantee you a buyer at the appraised—or at any—price.

CREATING DISTRIBUTION TECHNIQUES

In Chapter 12, we discussed our bias against voting as a method of making decisions among family members. There are other ways for your family to make decisions. Remember, it's the perception by all of a fair process that will minimize lingering resentments after you are done.

For example, when considering distribution of personal property, the decision is really that of the property's owner while he or she is alive. Yet, sometimes a parent wants input from her children about what personal items they would want after she passes away. This is not to say that she wants to give up control or that she guarantees she will follow all the expressed wishes of her children. Rather it is a way for a parent to feel that each of her children will inherit what he or she most wants, and it can also be an attempt to prevent sibling conflict after she is gone.

We saw one family successfully accomplish this with a well-considered plan. The mother had all her jewelry professionally appraised and then set it out on the dining room table along with information from the appraisal. She took her two daughters and her daughter-in-law out to lunch. Upon their return, each spent some individual time with their mother (-in-law) looking at all the jewelry and telling her what they wanted while the other two chatted on the porch. Because all the jewelry had been appraised, it was clear what the financial value was of each piece. Once all three had clarified their preferences, their mother, along with their father, made a decision about who would get what. While this may not be a perfect system for everyone, in this case it worked quite well.

SOME THOUGHTS ON DIVIDING
PERSONAL PROPERTY POST DEATH

After Mom and Dad are gone, there is often the matter of how to divide up their personal property. Even with a comprehensive estate plan, including wills and trusts, there are usually many personal items left behind that escape the scrutiny of the Probate Court and are not included in any instructions for the family.

The first order of business is to determine who "qualifies" as a stakeholder in the distribution of personal property. Sons and daughters may, in everyone's view, be entitled to an equal share of the financial value of furniture, jewelry, collectibles, etc. Yet others, regardless of their standing as heirs, may claim that they hold an interest in specific items. For example, Mom's business partner of 30 years may wish to take possession of any business-related items, such as expensive home-office furniture and equipment purchased by the company—and may even lay claim to awards and memorabilia from the early years. Some grandchildren may assert that they have special standing owing to their particularly close relationship with one or more of their grandparents. They may express interest in Nana's needlepoint and her recipe collection—items which often hold particular significance to loved ones. And life partners, who may not have legal standing despite their many years together, may assert the rights and interests of a spouse. Unmarried persons who leave behind a life partner without specifically providing for them can unwittingly create a legacy of conflict and untold misery if another family member challenges the partner's status.

A successful decision-making process may seem elusive when grieving relatives and others close to the deceased struggle to determine who is "entitled" to what. We find that the element of time is often essential. Even when there is good reason to empty Grandpa's house right away (maybe in order to take advantage of the spring real-estate market), it may make sense to find a neutral temporary home for the valued objects, like a rented storage unit, and set a time in the future for the decision-making process.

When it is time to make personal property distribution decisions, we find that the surviving adult children are most successful when they use the tools and skills we have discussed throughout this book. The decision-making process they design will likely provide the best results if it is structured to address everyone's interests, including the universally proclaimed interest of fairness. If the family's goal is to protect valued relationships, the process should allow everyone to be heard. Consider using a Consensus Building approach, and make distribution decisions with long-term consequences in mind.

As we discussed, although some items hold enormous emotional weight (regardless of their appraised value), it is often important to appraise any potentially valuable objects in order to provide the information needed regarding financial equity.

We have seen siblings successfully use a process that gives everyone a "fair" opportunity to select those objects they desire most. All the personal property should be on hand or listed on note cards (perhaps showing photos of the objects) set out or displayed in the meeting room. To get things going, everyone draws a Scrabble® tile, and the process begins with each person making one selection with the order of their turn being based on the alphabetical order of their tile. (Duplicate tiles are returned to the box, or the family can prepare a selection at the outset containing no duplicates.) Then, after each selection round, the person who selected an item first in that round goes to the bottom of the list so that everyone has a chance to be first. Tiles can be drawn again after each full cycle of everyone being first in a round. Selection rounds continue until all items have been claimed. In the end, if financial equality of each person's share of distributed items is important to the family (and it may not always be so), the total appraised value of each person's holdings can be equalized with cash from the estate or paid out between the siblings if the estate does not have any retained cash. Any plan to "equalize" needs to be made clear at the outset so that all participants can consider it in their selection decisions.

"Who Gets Grandma's Yellow Pie Plate?™ *A Guide to Passing on Personal Possessions"* is a terrific workbook published by the University of Minnesota Extension Service. In it, you'll find many more strategies for working through the emotional struggles around the distribution of your parents' (or your own) personal property—from determining together "what is fair" for your family to crafting distribution methods (such as auctions with "funny money") that factor in the emotional as well as the financial value of personal property. Many of our clients have found this to be a very valuable resource.

HONORING THE CAREGIVER

Despite your best efforts, it's almost inevitable that siblings' caregiving work will be unequal. So honor the worker bees. Give that brother or sister who takes such good care of Mom a vacation that the rest of you pay for, during which time you all manage Mom's care. And, don't forget to give recognition for the caregiver's work between vacations. You'd be amazed at how far an acknowledgement and a "thank you" can go— sincerely expressed appreciation can count a lot. Once you have spoken your appreciation, you may feel that you would actually like to demonstrate your sincerity with some unexpected generosity. You may even find that you want to give those caregivers a bit of an edge when selecting heirlooms or otherwise distributing items of value. We've seen this happen with some frequency.

THE DRIVING PROBLEM

In today's world, driving is more than transportation; it provides independence, autonomy, and a sense of belonging to the wider community. Needing to rely on others for appointments, meetings, and social connections can create a diminished sense of self, and a sense of dependency that can affect a person's life in untold ways.

Rather than getting into internal family battles of differing opinions regarding Mom's or Dad's safety as a driver, it may help to get a driving assessment by a legitimate third party. These services may be available in your area through the department of motor vehicles, the local police, community hospitals, etc. Specially trained occupational therapists can be especially helpful in providing comprehensive driving evaluations; they can recommend simple modifications or retraining for continued driving, if appropriate, or help your parent transition away from driving when it is time to do so. Don't forget to explore customized plans that evolve over time and limit driving (to particular roadways and/or times of day) in accordance with your parents' individual situation.

And if the "Dad can't drive anymore" moment comes, remember pride. Dad may need to hear the "no more" words from a non-family member, and he may need to actually give the keys to that person too. This could be Dad's doctor, a trusted friend, or his clergyperson.

For more information, see the driving resources listed under Guides for Adult Family Conversations on page 121.

SETTING UP A FAMILY BLOG OR PRIVATE WEBSITE

Today's technology makes it easy to communicate with family members and keep everyone in the loop. Often a parent acts as a hub of information for all family members. When Mom becomes less able to communicate or passes away, adult children may find themselves feeling unconnected to their siblings' lives. If Mom no longer is the conduit, you may not hear that your nephew had his wisdom teeth out or that your niece got into her first choice of colleges. Creating a blog or private website is a way some families keep in touch. It doesn't require much time and can be updated or read at any time, in any time zone.

INCLUDING PROFESSIONAL ADVISORS

As mediators, we very often suggest that other professionals be engaged in order to ensure that all family members are properly informed before making critical decisions, and we would urge you and your family to consider this as well. Sometimes complicated eldercare and estate issues require outside advisors.

Legal advice can be essential for a wide range of concerns, from protecting family assets to reviewing guardianship matters. It is important to understand your rights and the rights of others when your dispute lies "in the shadow of the law." Only an attorney can properly advise you about estate planning, trusts, powers of attorney, and so on. Legal strategies that are not ordinarily intuitive, like putting a vacation home into an LLC to avoid potential liabilities, can be proactive steps to preserve future family inheritances. Being well informed is, of course, the basis of good decision-making, and good legal information may be important to your process.

Beyond legal advice, if you are looking at matters related to estate planning, property transfers, and such, tax consequences can also be a concern. If so, appropriate financial professionals might be needed to advise your family during a decision-making process.

And of course, when a senior's health and safety are at issue, an assessment by a medical professional will be essential before important decisions can be made.

A geriatric care manager (GCM) can provide an objective assessment of an elder's daily needs and can offer advice on in-home support as well as residential facilities. Engaging a GCM can take the burden off a caregiver for determining what a parent needs and finding the appropriate resources. You can find a GCM in your area by visiting www.caremanager.org.

But remember that everyone has to agree with the choice of professionals to advise the family, unless participants wish to have individual advisors. In the end, informed consent is what matters most. All family members must have the information they need to make informed decisions.

DECIDING NOT TO DECIDE UNTIL INFORMATION IS GATHERED

Often families find that they are not ready to make decisions because additional information is essential for informed decision-making. If so, there's homework to be done—like interviewing real-estate agents, visiting assisted living facilities, calling elder service agencies and home care companies, and determining what community services are available for local transportation, etc.

"One-time" tasks, such as the research projects listed as homework above, can provide an opportunity for previously less-involved siblings to come through and contribute in a meaningful way. We worked with a family where one brother was able to download and analyze information on many local living facilities even though he lived out-of-state. He then prioritized which should be visited and, because he became part of the solution, he participated in some of those visits.

SETTING UP A PLAN FOR FUTURE MEETINGS IN PERSON OR BY PHONE

Back to technology: It is easy to set up free conference calls through online services or web chats. We've worked with families who have set a monthly or weekly check-in that allowed issues to be discussed regularly so everyone was in the loop before decisions were needed. And when decisions became necessary, everyone understood what had led up to the situation and all were invested in collaborating on the best solution. Some families have even set up a rotation for who chairs the call each time, so that the conversation runs smoothly, the burden is shared, and an agenda can be developed before the call to keep everyone on track.

WHEN FAMILIES CAN'T "DO IT THEMSELVES"— DISPUTE RESOLUTION ALTERNATIVES

There are a variety of professionals in the field of conflict resolution available to help you and your family move forward with decision-making. The field of dispute resolution can be confusing, so here's a brief overview:

MEDIATION—Mediation is *assisted negotiation* where a *neutral third party* helps his or her clients reach a mutually agreeable resolution. It is a voluntary and confidential process that allows families to maintain their privacy.

In mediation, nobody imposes a decision on you—you and the other participants maintain control of the outcome. Mediators don't tell you what to do, and they don't say who is right or wrong. Rather, they help you think about your interests and encourage you to be creative and to consider carefully all the possible options available to you. This generally leads to more satisfaction with the outcome and more durable agreements.

Mediators around the world are guided by the same five principles: confidentiality, neutrality of the mediator(s), voluntary participation by everyone, informed consent by all parties, and the upholding of self-determination (including lack of coercion) for all participants.

CONFLICT COACHING—In conflict coaching, a specialist in conflict resolution theory and practice helps an individual client to identify his or her interests and to develop strategies for working with others involved in a conflict. This is particularly useful when not all parties want to participate in mediation.

Conflict coaches work privately with individual clients to help them broaden the options available to them and their families with the goal of creating mutually acceptable solutions. This process involves helping clients identify and prioritize their goals and concerns, their wants and needs, their values and perceptions. Clients are also encouraged to consider the interests of their family members. Coaches teach their clients new skills for constructive communication and conflict resolution.

BINDING ARBITRATION—In binding arbitration, the arbitrator, who functions much like a judge, hears both (or all) sides of a conflict and then renders a decision on what should be done. Parties give up their right to participate in designing the final resolution; the arbitrator makes the decision for them and thereby limits the range of options available to the participants. The process is less expensive and time consuming than litigation, but as in litigation, parties give up control of the outcome.

LITIGATION—Sometimes a lawsuit is the only way or the best way to resolve a dispute. However, litigation is expensive and painful; court battles are lengthy and can be unsatisfying for both sides. And, even when lawsuits have been filed, most cases are ultimately settled before going in front of a judge. But the judicial system is there for us when we cannot resolve differences on our own (and, of course, when court approval is required, as in guardianship, conservatorship and probate matters).

—•—

As you can see, there are countless ways in which family members can resolve their disputes and make the important decisions that are needed in a time of transition. Adult siblings and aging parents bring years of experience and accumulated wisdom to their discussions. We hope you will see the above examples as just a sampling of the many ways in which family members have put their heads and hearts together to resolve their disputes, and to design their own solutions to the difficult and emotionally charged challenges they have faced as a family.

14

....

CONCLUSION

Family conflict is complicated. It pervades your life in ways that confound logic. A friend may be able to give you advice on how to resolve the situation—it sounds so easy to her. On the face of it, it does seem simple: Just tell your brother he needs to pull his weight. Just tell your sister that she needs to pay her share of the expenses to modify Dad's home. Just tell your mother you love her, but it's not safe for her to stay home alone. The reality, however, is not so simple. If you could just *do* it, you already would have, and you wouldn't be losing sleep at night. Family conflict is exhausting, and resolving it is no easy task. It takes patience, skill, and a bit of luck.

PUTTING YOUR NEW SKILLS TO WORK

In reading this guide, you've learned about some specific skills to help you approach the situation you are facing. Try using these skills to think through your circumstances and to design an approach customized to your family. <u>Listen</u> to what your family members are saying so you can understand their interests. Be genuinely curious, and <u>ask why</u> your siblings feel the way they do. And <u>show that you heard them</u>. Once they feel heard they will be better able to listen to you.

Whether you are struggling with issues related to caregiving, living situations, or sharing property, the necessary skills and the process are the same. Breaking through family dynamics is not easy—but remember, you are an expert on your family situation. You know the history, and you probably want what's best for everyone. But that doesn't mean you'll need to abandon your own interests, even if that's what you're used to doing. With your newly minted communication skills and your greater understanding of why people may act and react as they do, you are better prepared to begin a successful decision-making process and to move forward together.

Good Luck!

RESOURCES

SUGGESTED READING ON CONFLICT RESOLUTION

Fisher, R., & Ury, W. (1981). *Getting to Yes: Negotiating Agreement Without Giving In*. New York: Penguin.

Lazare, A. (2004). *On Apology*. New York: Oxford University Press.

Susskind, L. E., & Cruikshank, J. L. (2006). *Breaking Robert's Rules*. New York: Oxford University Press.

Stone, F., Patton, B., Heen, S. (1999). *Difficult Conversations: How to Discuss What Matters Most*. New York: Viking Penguin.

GUIDES FOR ADULT FAMILY CONVERSATIONS

At the Crossroads: Family Conversations about Alzheimer's Disease, Dementia & Driving from The Hartford Financial Services Group, Inc., and the MIT AgeLab. Free Booklet and Support Group Kit available. (www.thehartford.com/alzheimers, www.safedrivingforalifetime.com, and www.hartfordauto.thehartford.com/UI/Downloads/Crossroads.pdf)

Dugan, E. (2006). *The Driving Dilemma: The Complete Resource Guide for Older Drivers and Their Families*. New York: Collins.

Five Wishes from Aging with Dignity, a "living will that talks about. . . personal, emotional and spiritual needs as well as. . . medical wishes" and meets legal requirements in 42 states. (www.agingwithdignity.org/five-wishes.php)

We Need to Talk: Family Conversations with Older Drivers online seminar produced by AARP based on information created jointly by The Hartford and the MIT AgeLab. (www.aarp.org/home-garden/transportation/we_need_to_talk/)

Who Gets Grandma's Yellow Pie Plate?™ *Workbook: A Guide to Passing on Personal Possessions*. (1999). St. Paul, MN: University of Minnesota Extension Service. (Workbook, video, and other resources available from www.yellowpieplate.umn.edu)

AGING INFORMATION AND RESOURCES

Alzheimer's Association (www.alz.org)

American Association for Retired Persons—AARP (www.aarp.org)

American Bar Association Commission on Law & Aging (www.abanet.org/aging)

The Center for Social Gerontology (www.tcsg.org)

Elder Law Answers (www.elderlawanswers.com)

Eldercare Locator, a public service of the U.S. Administration on Aging (www.eldercare.gov)

National Academy of Elder Law Attorneys (www.naela.org)

National Association of Area Agencies on Aging (www.n4a.org/answers-on-aging)

National Association of Professional Geriatric Care Managers (www.napgcm.org or www.caremanager.org)

National Center on Elder Abuse, U.S. Administration on Aging (www.ncea.aoa.gov)

CAREGIVER RESOURCES

Berman, C. (2006). *Caring for Yourself While Caring for Your Aging Parents: How to Help, How to Survive.* Third edition. New York: Henry Holt and Company.

Coste, J. K. (2003). *Learning to Speak Alzheimer's: A Groundbreaking Approach for Everyone Dealing with the Disease.* Boston: Houghton Mifflin.

Mace, N. L., & Rabins P. V. (2006). *The 36 Hour Day: A Family Guide to Caring for Persons with Alzheimer Disease, Other Dementias, and Memory Loss in Later Life.* Fourth edition. Baltimore, Maryland: The Johns Hopkins University Press.

Caring.com—Information and resources for caregivers (www.caring.com)

Family Caregiver Handbook Website—Prepared by the MIT Workplace Center (http://web.mit.edu/workplacecenter/hndbk)

Losta Helping Hands—Free website to organize caregiving help (www.lotsahelpinghands.com)

National Family Caregivers Association (www.thefamilycaregiver.org)

Our Family Wizard—Subscription website designed for shared parenting, sometimes used by families to coordinate care for elder parents (www.ourfamilywizard.com)

ABOUT THE AUTHORS

Arline Kardasis, **Rikk Larsen**, **Crystal Thorpe** and **Blair Trippe** are mediators, trainers, and founding partners of Elder Decisions®, a division of Agreement Resources, LLC. Through mediation and conflict coaching, they help families resolve disputes around eldercare, property sharing, inheritance matters, and other adult family conflicts.

As a team, they have designed and delivered advanced trainings in elder mediation for mediators from around the United States and abroad. Individually and together, they have delivered workshops, seminars, and trainings in a wide spectrum of settings, including: Harvard Law School Program on Negotiation, the Sino-U.S. Judicial Mediation Exchange Program, the Judges' Institute at the Connecticut Probate Assembly, the American Bar Association, the National Association of Professional Geriatric Care Managers, the National Academy of Elder Law Attorneys, the Association for Conflict Resolution, the Dartmouth-Hitchcock Medical Center's conference on Alzheimer's disease, and the Map Through the Maze Conferences of the Alzheimer's Association.

All of the Elder Decisions partners have served on Subcommittees for the Massachusetts Trial Court's Standing Committee on Dispute Resolution.

ARLINE KARDASIS served as a founding tri-chair of the Elder Decision-Making and Conflict Resolution Section of the Association for Conflict Resolution, and she is the former Vice President of the Board of Directors of the Association for Conflict Resolution-New England Chapter. She received her BA in Political Science and Urban Studies from Boston University and her MAT in Secondary Education from Simmons College.

RIKK LARSEN is a life coach and an estate settlement specialist as well as a mediator and trainer. He has written extensively about adult family conflict. Rikk is a former court case coordinator for the Harvard Mediation Program. He received his BA in Economics from Williams College and his MBA from Harvard Business School.

CRYSTAL THORPE has over ten years of experience in the corporate and non-profit sectors in the areas of training, human resources, quality assurance, and consulting. She now focuses exclusively on conflict resolution for families and workplaces. She holds an MSW and an MBA from Boston College and an undergraduate degree in Cognitive Science/Psycholinguistics, magna cum laude, from Brown University.

BLAIR TRIPPE is a former member of the Board of Directors of the Association for Conflict Resolution-New England Chapter. In addition to her work as a mediator and trainer, Blair is a consultant to family businesses around issues of succession planning and governance. She earned an MBA from the Kellogg School of Management at Northwestern University, a BA in Psychology from Connecticut College, and a Certificate in Family Business Advising from the Family Firm Institute.

14398673R00070

Made in the USA
Lexington, KY
26 March 2012